The Pocket Encyclopedia of World Aircraft in Color

BOMBERS

PATROL AND TRANSPORT AIRCRAFT

1939–45

The Pocket Encyclopedia
of World Aircraft in Color

BOMBERS
PATROL AND TRANSPORT AIRCRAFT
1939–45

by
KENNETH MUNSON

Illustrated by
JOHN W. WOOD

Norman Dinnage
Frank Friend
Brian Hiley
William Hobson
Tony Mitchell
Jack Pelling

THE MACMILLAN COMPANY

First published in 1969
Copyright © 1969 Blandford Press Ltd.

Library of Congress Catalog Card Number 77–92035

First Printing
Color printed by The Ysel Press, Deventer, Holland
Text printed and books bound in England by
Richard Clay (The Chaucer Press), Ltd., Bungay, Suffolk

PREFACE

So many different types of aeroplane, old and new, conventional and bizarre, were involved in the war of 1939-45 that any selection for a volume of this size must necessarily be an arbitrary one. In this initial presentation, therefore, the selection has been governed primarily by the operational importance of the aircraft concerned, although some types have other claims for inclusion.

As before, our collective thanks are due to Ian D. Huntley for his invaluable specific knowledge and general guidance in the matter of aircraft colouring and markings. Also of considerable assistance have been the three invaluable volumes of *Markings and Camouflage Systems of Luftwaffe Aircraft in World War II*, by Karl Ries Jr. Grateful acknowledgment is also made of items published at various times by *The Aeromodeller*, *Ai Review*, *Air Pictorial*, *Aviation Magazine International*, the *Journal of the American Aviation Historical Society*, *Flying Review International*, *Interconair*, the *IPMS Magazine* and Profile Publications Ltd. Individual help was again kindly given by Lt.-Col. N. Kindberg, of the Royal Swedish Air Force, and Jørgen Lundø, of Politikens Forlag, Copenhagen. Finally, my thanks go, as always, to Pamela Matthews for her considerable help in the preparation and checking of the manuscript.

Kenneth Munson

May 1969

INTRODUCTION

Most of the European nations involved in the war of 1939-45 had, during the latter half of the 1930s, embarked upon plans to expand and re-equip their air forces with more modern combat types. The natural process of evolution of new military aircraft was hastened by a belated recognition of the potential danger which existed in the form of the increasing might of the German *Luftwaffe*. However, by the outbreak of World War 2 Germany still possessed the strongest and most modern air force in Europe.

Germany had been categorically forbidden by the 1919 Treaty of Versailles to manufacture military aeroplanes, although the construction of light civil aircraft was allowed to continue on a modest scale. Most of the restrictions imposed by the Versailles Treaty were withdrawn in the 1926 Paris Air Agreement, and from then onward there began the re-establishment of a substantial aircraft industry, not only within Germany itself but in the form of new factories set up in Switzerland, the U.S.S.R. and elsewhere. The national airline, *Deutsche Lufthansa*, and the re-created *Luftsportverband*, ostensibly a private flying organisation, acted as a political cloak for new para-military activities whereby new bombers, fighters and transport aircraft were developed under the guise of fast 'air taxis', 'sporting' single-seaters and high-speed mailplanes. New military prototypes commonly appeared bearing civilian registration letters, but their quasi-civilian purpose was fairly apparent, and after Hitler came to power in 1933 little further attempt was made to preserve the pretence, although the practice of allocating civil registration marks to military prototypes continued. In 1935 the existence of the new *Luftwaffe* was confirmed officially when it was announced that *Reichsmarschall* Hermann Goering, the former Air Minister, had been appointed as its new Commander-in-Chief. After the German occupation of Austria in 1938 factories in that country were also utilised for the production of aeroplanes for the *Luftwaffe* and the output of combat aircraft for the German air force rose from some 300 a month at the end of 1935 to more than 1,000 a month by September 1939.

By comparison, the expansion programme embarked upon by the RAF before World War 2 was both modest and slow. Until 1936 the bomber force was composed principally of obsolescent biplanes or slow, ponderous monoplanes; but then, with the introduction of the 'shadow factory' programme, the extensive re-equipment of the RAF with more modern combat aircraft began, with the British motor-car industry geared to turn out aeroplanes to supplement those produced by the aircraft industry. In addition, substantial numbers of American types were ordered for the RAF by the British Purchasing Mission which visited the U.S.A. in 1938. Despite this augmented programme, however, on 3 September 1939 the RAF had no four-engined heavy bombers in service, and the total number of twin-engined medium bombers on charge at that time comprised only 226 Hampdens, 179 Wellingtons and 207 Whitleys. Of these, the Whitleys were already virtually obsolete, and only 169 Hampdens and 160 Wellingtons were with front-line squadrons. The light day bomber situation was slightly better, at least numerically, for there were 1,075 twin-engined Blenheims and 1,133 single-engined Battles on strength; but only half of these were with operational units, and the Battle was later to prove something of a disappointment. The Fleet Air Arm was in an even poorer state, its most modern fighter in September 1939 being the Sea Gladiator biplane. Seven new aircraft carriers had been ordered in 1938, but for the first three years or more of the war the best British torpedo-bomber-reconnaissance types that they had aboard them were also slow, vulnerable biplanes, and it is no small tribute to the quality of such aircraft as the Fairey Swordfish that it was capable of being flown with distinction and to good military effect for the major part of the war. Poland, France and the smaller European nations were, like Britain, still in the midst of their respective modernisation programmes when the war struck them. Each had excellent new types under development, but all too few were actually in service by the time they were needed.

The civil war which had broken out in Spain in 1936 had afforded an ideal opportunity for several European powers to send detachments of combat aircraft to that country, where they could gain valuable operational experience under genuine battle conditions. In the light of future events this was to prove something of a mixed blessing. In Spain, where they were generally opposed by aircraft older or technically inferior to those which they were flying themselves, the pilots of Germany's *Legion Condor* and Italy's *Aviazione Legionaria* were usually able to dispose of any aerial opposition with comparative ease. Bomber squadrons in particular were able to carry out raids with little or no fighter escort, since their opponents were either too few, too slow or too old to interrupt their progress seriously. The successful application of these tactics in Spain not unnaturally led the *Luftwaffe* to pursue similar tactics at the outset of World War 2, and in the initial advances across eastern and western Europe this policy continued to prove successful.

After the Dunkirk evacuation and the fall of France in 1940, the *Luftwaffe* began to increase its campaign of bombing raids against the United Kingdom as a preliminary softening-up process prior to the intended invasion of England. However, in the late summer of 1940 the *Luftwaffe* suffered its first serious defeat in the air when, in the Battle of Britain, operating without ground support and against superior fighter opposition, it failed to achieve the measure of air superiority required to allow the bomber force to achieve its objective. The success achieved by the RAF in the Battle of Britain gave the Allied air forces a valuable initial breathing space in which they were able to recover and remuster their strength before preparing first to withstand the continued German *blitzkrieg* and then to mount their own counter-bombing offensive.

Meanwhile, in June 1940 Italy had entered the war on the German side, and although the *Regia Aeronautica* possessed rather less modern warplanes than the *Luftwaffe*, it was still numerically a force to be reckoned with, having nearly 1,000 bombers and over 750 reconnaissance, transport and non-combatant types in its overall inventory. Germany did not immediately learn the lesson of the Battle of Britain, although one outcome was a marked increase in the defensive armament of her bomber fleet. The *Luftwaffe* continued daylight bombing attacks for quite some time afterwards; had it turned over immediately to a night bombing offensive while British night defences were still inadequate, the story might well have been a different one. As it was, Germany lost around 2,000 aircraft and 5,000 aircrew in continued daylight attacks before switching to a night offensive. For a short time during 1940-41 Italian bombers based in Belgium gave some support to the *Luftwaffe* during day and night raids on British targets, but they achieved little success in this quarter, and were soon required to return home for operations in the Mediterranean area or in North Africa. A serious blow was dealt to the Italian war machine in November 1940 by the Fleet Air Arm, which brought off a remarkably successful attack on the Italian Fleet at Taranto, inflicting losses and damage almost as serious in their effect as those incurred just over a year later by the U.S. Navy when its ships at Pearl Harbor were attacked by the Japanese Naval Air Force. With one or two exceptions, Italian bombers of the war period were not an outstandingly successful breed. The only four-engined Italian bomber, the Piaggio P.108B, served only in small numbers, and, coincidentally, none of the multi-engined strategic bombers developed by Germany and Japan were successful operationally.

One of the biggest single factors in the ultimate downfall of Naziism was undoubtedly Hitler's decision in 1941 to invade the U.S.S.R. The Soviet Air Force had been another participant in the Spanish Civil War of 1936-39, and in 1938-39 was also engaged against the air forces of Japan during the Siberian border disputes. A major expansion and re-equipment programme for the Soviet Air Force was put in hand as a result of these campaigns, but at the time of the German invasion few new aircraft had been developed and put into service, and the Soviet Air Force, although strong numerically, did not possess large numbers of modern combat aircraft. The gap was bridged to a considerable extent after March 1941, when the U.S. Congress gave approval to the Lend-Lease Act, which permitted the donation of American aircraft to the Allied powers. By the end of 1942 several of the new Soviet-designed types had become available in quantity. Most of these were fighters or ground-attack aircraft; the bomber force was made up largely of the Ilyushin DB-3F and Tupolev SB-2, supplemented by such U.S. medium bomber types as the Douglas A-20 and North American B-25.

The U.S.A. had always been overtly sympathetic to the Allied cause, and the substantial numbers of American aircraft ordered before the war by the British Purchasing Commission were now augmented still further by the diversion to Britain of unfulfilled

French orders and by further supplies made under the Lend-Lease Act. When the U.S.A. itself was forced in December 1941 to become an active participant in the war the already large work load placed upon the American aircraft industry was increased by many more huge orders for combat aircraft for its own services, and several newly developed types were also earmarked for production. By a coincidence, U.S. and British strategists had each pursued, according to their own convictions, the evolution of specialised warplanes for certain roles which they considered vital. Fortuitously, these types largely complemented rather than overlapped one another when it came to the matter of pooling British and American production resources in a common war effort. Thus, the major U.S. effort was concentrated upon the production of long-range heavy bombers, patrol aircraft and transports. Nevertheless, considerable numbers of medium and light bombers were among the early supplies of Lend-Lease aircraft supplied to Britain and the U.S.S.R. The U.S. industry undertook the mass production of virtually all the transport aircraft required by the Allied powers, and at the outset nearly one-third of the total U.S. productive effort was devoted to the manufacture of transport types. The subsequent intermixture of aircraft between Britain and the U.S.A. resulted in a more comprehensive array of combat types than either country could probably have achieved by itself.

Japan's action in precipitating the U.S. entry into the war proved to be the final undoing of the Axis powers. The aircraft in service with the Japanese Army and Naval Air Forces at this time, like those of the other combatants, were largely those that had begun to enter service in the middle and late 1930s. Japan, too, had tested her military equipment under operational conditions and against a technically inferior adversary during conflicts throughout the 1930s with China and, later, with Siberia. The Japanese entry into the war was heralded by bomber types of the Japanese Naval Air Force, which flew from their parent aircraft carriers to attack the U.S. Fleet in Pearl Harbor early on the morning of 7 December 1941. Japan's subsequent activity during the war can be divided broadly into that on the mainland of south-east Asia, carried out chiefly by the Army Air Force, and that among the numerous island groups in the south-west Pacific, which was largely the responsibility of the Naval Air Force. So long as it retained its aircraft carriers, the Japanese Fleet was a formidable adversary; but, as the war progressed and its carrier fleet was gradually diminished and ultimately demolished, its power in the Pacific was reduced to negligible proportions. The Japanese Army overran the southern mainland of Asia so quickly at the outset of its offensive that its air force became very thinly spread over the vast area which it now had to cover, and eventually home production was unable to keep pace with even the normal combat wastage of aircraft for each service. America's vast output of transport aircraft was of particular value in south-east Asia, although naturally they figured largely in every major campaign of the war. Especially noteworthy was the maintenance of the supply routes across the Himalayas between India and China, without which the Allied forces in that theatre would have been hard pressed to maintain or advance their position. In April 1942 General 'Jimmy' Doolittle's small force of Mitchell bombers, taking off from the aircraft carrier *Hornet* to carry out a bombing attack on Tokyo, made world headlines. This operation was noteworthy for the fact that it took place at all, even though it was more of a morale-booster than an operation of great military value; but two months later, in June 1942, Japan suffered a really serious defeat in the Battle of Midway Island, in the course of which she lost four aircraft carriers and over 250 aircraft. The Battle of Midway was as much a key turning-point of the war in the Pacific as the Battle of Britain had been in the war in Europe.

Within a year of Pearl Harbor the number of aircraft in service with the U.S. forces had trebled, and most of this strength was serving abroad, to such an extent that it became necessary for the USAAF to loan some of its aircraft to the U.S. Navy so that the latter could maintain adequate maritime patrols over American home waters. One of the first steps taken by the USAAF was the establishment of the U.S. Eighth Air Force at bases in the United Kingdom, from where its Fortress and Liberator four-engined bombers could join with the RAF's Stirling, Halifax and Lancaster 'heavies' in carrying out round-the-clock day and night bombing of German targets. In the autumn of 1942 part of the Eighth was detached to form the basis of the U.S. Twelfth Air Force in North Africa. In 1943, after the successful conclusion of the North African campaign, first Sicily and then Italy were invaded. The bombing offensive against Germany continued, now with frequent thousand-bomber raids; and smaller, faster types, such as the Mosquito, were making their presence felt, both in the precision bombing of specialised targets and as pathfinders for the bigger bombers. Mosquitos also performed a considerable amount of photographic reconnaissance work, bringing back valuable intelligence pictures of the damage inflicted by the bombers. By this time, the British Fleet Air Arm was at last beginning to receive more modern monoplane fighters and bombers of British design, to augment the American types received earlier under Lend-Lease arrangements. One effect of the sustained bombing of Germany was the wholesale recall of *Luftwaffe* fighter squadrons from other fronts, from which they could ill be spared, to defend the German homeland; moreover, defensive fighters were now outnumbering bombers in the overall *Luftwaffe* establishment. Nevertheless, by cutting its reserves to negligible proportions, the *Luftwaffe* was still able to claim a first-line strength in mid-1943 of around 4,000 aircraft.

On 8 September 1943 the Italian forces under the command of Marshal Badoglio surrendered to the Allies, and the aircraft based in Italy became divided into two opposing camps. Those in that half of Italy which had still not been reached by the Allied advance were formed into the *Aviazione della Repubblica Sociale Italiana* and continued to fight alongside the *Luftwaffe*, while those in southern Italy became known as the Italian Co-Belligerent Air Force, which continued to fight with mixed Italian, American and British types on behalf of the Allied cause. Towards the end of 1943 the forthcoming invasion of the Continent was fore-shadowed by the setting up in November of the Allied Second Tactical Air Force, and by the increase in ground-attack raids against enemy targets. By the time the invasion came on 6 June 1944, day and night raids upon German-held targets were being made with comparative impunity, and valuable diversionary raids were made to distract enemy defence resources away from the invasion area. The invasion of Normandy itself involved one of the largest single troop movements in history, in which even the prodigious numbers of American transport aircraft were augmented by the use of many older bomber types to act as tugs for the troop-carrying gliders.

The invasion did not bring any decrease in the mass bombing

of German industrial areas, and among the later weapons devised for attacking such specialised targets as railway centres and viaducts was the tremendous 22,000-lb 'Grand Slam' bomb, which could be carried only by specially modified Lancasters. Germany, too, produced some last-minute weapons in the form of the *Vergeltungswaffen* (Reprisal Weapons) V1 and V2. The V1 flying bombs constituted a slight setback for a time in the autumn of 1944, but their measure was soon taken by the RAF's piston-engined Tempest and jet-engined Meteor fighters. Repeated attacks on their factories and launching sites finally disposed of the menace both from the V1 and from the V2 rocket missiles, which were used against Britain for a time during 1944-45. The hard-hit German aviation industry achieved a partial respite by an extensive dispersal of its factories and by setting up new plants underground, almost exclusively by now for the production of defensive fighters; but even these new aircraft were prevented from entering service in appreciable numbers by the continued attentions of Allied bombers to their factories and airfields. Among the types whose careers were thus affected was the Arado Ar 234, the first jet bomber to go into service anywhere in the world. The *Luftwaffe* suffered a final indignity by having its surviving aircraft virtually grounded for lack of fuel during the closing weeks of the European war.

From the end of 1944, once the end of the war in Europe was in sight, South-East Asia Command underwent a considerable expansion preparatory to a final all-out offensive in the Pacific theatre. After the end of the European war some twenty bomber squadrons were nominated as part of a new 'Tiger Force' which was to be dispatched to the Far East to supplement the existing bomber force; but this formation was still working up to operational level when Japan surrendered.

The successful American campaigns to recapture the Philippines and Marianas island groups in 1944 had marked the beginning of the final stage of the Pacific war, for after these actions Japanese sea power in the area was virtually non-effective, and the fanatical suicide attacks engaged in by Japanese Army and Navy pilots in their explosive-laden aircraft provided only a temporary, if serious, setback. The recapture of the Marianas islands of Saipan, Tinian and Guam by the U.S. Naval and Marine forces had at last given the Army Air Force the forward bases that it needed for its new B-29 Superfortress bombers to mount a regular series of attacks against targets within Japan itself, and in November 1944 over 100 Superfortresses raided Tokyo. Apart from the tremendous damage inflicted by such raids, the waters around Japan were heavily laid with mines to cut off external supply routes by sea. The last significant gestures by *Kamikaze* suicide pilots were made at Iwo Jima and Okinawa; and finally, it fell to the Superfortress to become the instrument for delivering the two atomic bombs on Hiroshima and Nagasaki which brought World War 2 to its end in August 1945.

THE COLOUR PLATES

As an aid to identification, the eighty colour plates which follow have been arranged in an essentially visual order, within the broad sequence: biplanes, single-engined monoplanes and multi-engined monoplanes. The sole rocket-powered aircraft appears last of all. The reference number of each type corresponds to the appropriate text matter, and an index to all types illustrated appears on pp. 162-3.

The 'split' plan view, adopted to give both upper and lower surface markings within a single plan outline, depicts the colour scheme appearing above and below either the port half or starboard half of the aircraft, according to whichever aspect is shown in the side elevation. This should be borne in mind when studying, for example, the plan views of U.S. aircraft, on which, normally, the national insignia appear only on the port upper and starboard lower surfaces of the wings.

1

Saunders-Roe-built Walrus II of No. 711 Squadron Fleet Air Arm, *ca.* spring
1941. *Engine:* One 775 h.p. Bristol Pegasus VI radial. *Span:* 45 ft. 10 in.
(13.97 m.). *Length:* 37 ft. 7 in. (11.46 m.). *Height:* 15 ft. 3 in. (4.65 m.).
Normal take-off weight: 7,200 lb. (3,266 kg.). *Maximum speed:* 135 m.p.h.
(217 km./hr.) at 4,750 ft. (1,448 m.). *Operational ceiling:* 18,500 ft. (5,639 m.).
Range: 600 miles (966 km.). *Armament:* One 0.303 in. Vickers K gun on Scarff
ring in each of bow and mid-upper positions; light load of small bombs or
depth charges beneath lower wings.

17

ALBACORE (U.K.)

2

Fairey Albacore I of No. 826 Squadron, HMS *Formidable*, spring 1941. *Engine:* One 1,065 h.p. Bristol Taurus II radial. *Span:* 50 ft. 0 in. (15.24 m.). *Length:* 39 ft. 10 in. (12.14 m.). *Height:* 14 ft. 2¼ in. (4.32 m.). *Normal take-off weight:* 10,460 lb. (4,745 kg.). *Maximum speed:* 161 m.p.h. (259 km./hr.) at 4,000 ft. (1,219 m.). *Operational ceiling:* 20,700 ft. (6,310 m.). *Range with torpedo:* 930 miles (1,497 km.). *Armament:* One 0.303 in. machine-gun in starboard wing and two 0.303 in. Vickers K guns in rear cockpit; one 1,610 lb. (730 kg.) torpedo beneath fuselage or up to 2,000 lb. (907 kg.) or bombs beneath lower wings.

3

Fairey Swordfish II (unit unidentified) of the Fleet Air Arm, July 1944. *Engine:* One 690 h.p. Bristol Pegasus IIIM.3 radial. *Span:* 45 ft. 6 in. (13.87 m.). *Length:* 35 ft. 8 in. (10.87 m.). *Height:* 12 ft. 4 in. (3.76 m.). *Maximum take-off weight:* 7,510 lb. (3,406 kg.). *Maximum speed:* 138 m.p.h. (222 km./hr.) at 5,000 ft. (1,524 m.). *Operational ceiling:* 19,250 ft. (5,867 m.). *Typical range:* 546 miles (879 km.). *Armament:* One 0.303 in. Vickers machine-gun in upper engine cowling and one 0.303 in. Lewis or Vickers K gun in rear cockpit; eight 60 lb. (27 kg.). rocket projectiles beneath lower wings.

NORSEMAN (Canada)

4

Noorduyn UC-64A Norseman of the USAAF, summer 1944. *Engine:* One 600 h.p. Pratt & Whitney R-1340-AN-1 Wasp radial. *Span:* 51 ft. 8 in. (15.75 m.). *Length:* 31 ft. 9 in. (9.68 m.). *Height:* 10 ft. 1 in. (3.07 m.). *Maximum take-off weight:* 7,400 lb. (3,357 kg.). *Maximum speed:* 165 m.p.h. (266 km./hr.) at 5,000 ft. (1,524 m.). *Operational ceiling:* 17,000 ft. (5,182 m.). *Typical range:* 600 miles (966 km.). *Armament:* None.

5

Westland Lysander ASR IIIA of No. 277 Squadron RAF, southern England, summer 1942. *Engine:* One 870 h.p. Bristol Mercury 30 radial. *Span:* 50 ft. 0 in. (15.24 m.). *Length:* 30 ft. 6 in. (9.30 m.). *Height:* 14 ft. 6 in. (4.42 m.). *Maximum take-off weight:* 6,318 lb. (2,866 kg.). *Maximum speed:* 212 m.p.h. (341 km./hr.) at 5,000 ft. (1,524 m.). *Operational ceiling:* 21,500 ft. (6,553 m.). *Typical range:* 500 miles (805 km.). *Armament:* One 0.303 in. Browning machine-gun in each wheel fairing; two more on movable mounting in rear of cabin.

FIESELER Fi 156 (Germany)

6

Fieseler Fi 156C-2 *Storch*, North Africa, *ca.* spring 1941. *Engine:* One 240 h.p. Argus As 10C inverted-Vee type. *Span:* 46 ft. 9 in. (14.25 m.). *Length:* 32 ft. 5¾ in. (9.90 m.). *Height:* 10 ft. 0 in. (3.05 m.). *Normal take-off weight:* 2,923 lb. (1,326 kg.). *Maximum speed:* 109 m.p.h. (175 km./hr.) at sea level. *Operational ceiling:* 16,700 ft. (5,090 m.). *Maximum range with standard fuel:* 239 miles (385 km.). *Armament:* One 7.9 mm. MG 15 machine-gun in rear of cabin.

BERIEV MBR-2 (U.S.S.R.)

7

Beriev MBR-2 of the VVS-VMF (Soviet Naval Aviation), unit and date not determined. *Engine:* One 750 h.p. Mikulin AM-34N Vee type. *Span:* 62 ft. 4 in. (19.00 m.). *Length:* 44 ft. 3½ in. (13.50 m.). *Height:* approximately 14 ft. 9 in. (4.40 m.). *Maximum take-off weight:* 9,359 lb. (4,245 kg.). *Maximum speed:* 171 m.p.h. (275 km./hr.) at 6,560 ft. (2,000 m.). *Operatioñal ceiling:* 16,080 ft. (4,900 m.). *Maximum range:* 932 miles (1,500 km.). *Armament:* One 7.62 mm. PV-1 machine-gun in open bow position and one 7.62 mm. ShKAS machine-gun in dorsal turret; up to 661 lb. (300 kg.) of bombs, mines or depth charges beneath the wings.

23

AICHI D3A (Japan)

8

Aichi D3A1 Model 11 from the aircraft carrier *Zuikaku*, southern Pacific 1941–42.
Engine: One 1,075 h.p. Mitsubishi Kinsei 44 radial. *Span:* 47 ft. 1½ in. (14.365 m.).
Length: 33 ft. 5⅜ in. (10,195 m.). *Height:* 10 ft. 11⅞ in. (3.35 m.). *Normal take-off
weight:* 8,047 lb. (3,650 kg.). *Maximum speed:* 242 m.p.h. (389 km./hr.) at
7,612 ft. (2,320 m.). *Operational ceiling:* 31,170 ft (9,500 m.). *Normal range:*
1,131 miles (1,820 km.). *Armament:* One 7.7 mm. machine-gun in each wing
and one in rear cockpit; one 551 lb. (250 kg.) and two 130 lb. (60 kg.) bombs.

ARADO Ar 196 (Germany)

9

Arado Ar 196A-3 of 2/*Bordfl. Gruppe* 196, southern Italy, 1942. *Engine:* One 960 h.p. BMW 132K radial. *Span:* 40 ft. 8⅛ in. (12.40 m.). *Length:* 36 ft. 1⅛ in. (11.00 m.). *Height:* 14 ft. 4⅜ in. (4.40 m.). *Normal take-off weight:* 8,223 lb. (3,730 kg.). *Maximum speed:* 193 m.p.h. (310 km./hr.) at 13,120 ft. (4,000 m.). *Operational ceiling:* 23,000 ft. (7,020 m.). *Range:* 665 miles (1,070 km.). *Armament:* One 20 mm. MG FF cannon in each wing, two 7.9 mm. MG 17 machine-guns in rear cockpit and one in front fuselage; one 110 lb. (50 kg.) bomb beneath each wing.

NAKAJIMA B5N (Japan)

10

Nakajima B5N2 operating from the carrier *Zuikaku* during the Battle of the Coral Sea, May 1942. *Engine:* One 970 h.p. Nakajima Sakae 11 radial. *Span:* 50 ft. 11 in. (15.52 m.). *Length:* 33 ft. 9½ in. (10.30 m.). *Height:* 12 ft. 1⅜ in. (3.70 m.). *Maximum take-off weight:* 9,039 lb. (4,100 kg.). *Maximum speed:* 235 m.p.h. (378 km./hr.) at 11,810 ft. (3,600 m.). *Operational ceiling:* 27,100 ft. (8,260 m.). *Maximum range:* 1,075 miles (1,730 km.). *Armament:* Two 7.7 mm. machine-guns in upper engine cowling and one or two in rear cockpit; one 1,764 lb. (800 kg.) torpedo, or three 551 lb. (250 kg.) or 132 lb. (60 kg.) bombs, beneath the fuselage.

11
Douglas SBD-5 Dauntless of Squadron VB-5, USS *Yorktown*, August/
September 1943. *Engine:* One 1,200 h.p. Wright R-1820-60 Cyclone radial.
Span: 41 ft. 6 in. (12.65 m.). *Length:* 33 ft. 0 in. (10.06 m.). *Height:* 12 ft. 11 in.
(3.94 m.). *Maximum take-off weight:* 10,700 lb. (4,853 kg.). *Maximum speed:*
252 m.p.h. (406 km./hr.) at 13,800 ft. (4,200 m.). *Operational ceiling:* 24,300 ft.
(7,400 m.). *Range with 1,000 lb. (454 kg.) bomb load:* 1,115 miles (1,794 km.).
Armament: Two 0.50 in. machine-guns in front of fuselage, and two 0.30 in.
guns in rear cockpit; one 1,000 lb. (454 kg.) or 500 lb. (227 kg.) bomb beneath
fuselage, or two 100 lb. (45 kg.) bombs or two 250 lb. (113 kg.) depth charges
beneath the wings.   27

YOKOSUKA D4Y (Japan)

12

Yokosuka D4Y2 Model 12 *Suisei* of No. 107 Attack Squadron, No. 503 Air Corps, JNAF, 1944. *Engine:* One 1,400 h.p. Aichi Atsuta 32 inverted-Vee type. *Span:* 37 ft. 8½ in. (11.49 m.). *Length:* 33 ft. 6⅜ in. (10.22 m.). *Height:* 12 ft. 3¼ in. (3.74 m.). *Maximum take-off weight:* 9,597 lb. (4,353 kg.). *Maximum speed:* 366 m.p.h. (589 km./hr.) at 17,225 ft. (5,250 m.). *Operational ceiling:* 35,170 ft. (10,720 m.). *Normal range:* 749 miles (1,205 km.). *Armament:* Two 7.7 mm. machine-guns in upper engine cowling and one in rear cockpit; one 551 lb. (250 kg.) bomb internally and one 66 lb. (30 kg.) bomb beneath each wing.

13
Eastern-built TBM-3 Avenger of Air Group 38, US Navy, August 1945. *Engine:*
One 1,900 h.p. Wright R-2600-20 Cyclone radial. *Span:* 54 ft. 2 in. (16.51 m.).
Length: 40 ft. 0⅛ in. (12.19 m.). *Height:* 16 ft. 5 in. (5.00 m.). *Maximum take-off
weight:* 18,250 lb. (8,278 kg.). *Maximum speed:* 267 m.p.h. (430 km./hr.) at
15,000 ft. (4,572 m.). *Operational ceiling:* 23,400 ft. (7,132 m.). *Maximum range:*
2,530 miles (4,072 km.). *Armament:* One 0.50 in. machine-gun in each wing
and one in dorsal turret; one 0.30 in. machine-gun in upper engine cowling and
one in ventral position; one 22-in. torpedo or one 2,000 lb. (907 kg.) bomb
internally. Provision for rocket projectiles beneath each wing.

SUKHOI Su-2 (U.S.S.R.)

14

Sukhoi Su-2 of an unidentified operational training unit of the Soviet Air Force, 1943. *Engine:* One 1,000 h.p. M-88B radial. *Span:* 46 ft. 11 in. (14.30 m.). *Length:* 33 ft. 7½ in. (10.25 m.). *Height:* approx. 12 ft. 3¾ in. (3.75 m.). *Maximum take-off weight:* 9,645 lb. (4,375 kg.). *Maximum speed:* 283 m.p.h. (455 km./ hr.) at 14,435 ft. (4,400 m.). *Operational ceiling:* 28,870 ft. (8,800 m.). *Range with 882 lb. (400 kg.) bomb load:* 746 miles (1,200 km.). *Armament:* Four 7.62 mm. ShKAS machine-guns in wings and one in dorsal turret; up to 1,323 lb. (600 kg.) of bombs.

HELLDIVER (U.S.A.)

15

Curtiss SB2C-1C of Squadron VB-8, USS *Bunker Hill*, June 1944. *Engine:*
One 1,700 h.p. Wright R-2600-8 Cyclone radial. *Span:* 49 ft. 8⅝ in. (15.15 m.).
Length: 36 ft. 8 in. (11.18 m.). *Height:* 14 ft. 9 in. (4.50 m.). *Normal take-off
weight:* 14,760 lb. (6,695 kg.). *Maximum speed:* 281 m.p.h. (452 km./hr.) at
12,400 ft. (3,780 m.). *Operational ceiling:* 24,700 ft. (7,529 m.). *Maximum
range:* 1,895 miles (3,050 km.). *Armament:* One 20 mm. cannon in each wing
and two 0.30 in. machine-guns in rear of cabin; one 1,000 lb. (454 kg.) bomb
internally.

NAKAJIMA B6N (Japan)

16

Nakajima B6N2 *Tenzan* of the 752nd Air Corps, JNAF, June 1944. *Engine:* One 1,850 h.p. Mitsubishi Kasei 25 radial. *Span:* 48 ft. 10⅜ in. (14.90 m.). *Length:* 35 ft. 7½ in. (10.86 m.). *Height:* 12 ft. 5⅝ in. (3.80 m.). *Maximum take-off weight:* 12,456 lb. (5,650 kg.). *Maximum speed:* 299 m.p.h. (482 km./hr.) at 16,080 ft. (4,900 m.). *Operational ceiling:* 29,660 ft. (9,040 m.). *Maximum range:* 1,644 miles (2,646 km.). *Armament:* One 7.7 mm. machine-gun in port wing, one in rear cockpit and one in ventral position; one 1,764 lb. (800 kg.) torpedo or six 220 lb. (100 kg.) bombs beneath the fuselage.

17

Fairey Barracuda II of No. 829 Squadron, HMS *Victorious* during attack on the *Tirpitz*, July 1944. *Engine:* One 1,600 h.p. Rolls-Royce Merlin 32 Vee type. *Span:* 49 ft. 2 in. (14.99 m.). *Length:* 39 ft. 9 in. (12.12 m.). *Height:* 15 ft. 1 in. (4.60 m.). *Maximum take-off weight:* 14,100 lb. (6,395 kg.). *Maximum speed:* 228 m.p.h. (367 km/hr.) at 1,750 ft. (533 m.). *Operational ceiling:* 16,600 ft. (5,060 m.). *Range with torpedo:* 686 miles (1,104 km.). *Armament:* Two 0.303 in. Vickers K guns in rear of cabin; one 1,620 lb. (735 kg.) torpedo or one 1,000 lb. (454 kg.) bomb beneath fuselage, or four 450 lb. (204 kg.) depth charges or six 250 lb. (113 kg.) bombs beneath the wings.

BATTLE (U.K.)

18

Fairey Battle II of No. 218 Squadron, after its re-formation in the UK ,in June 1940. *Engine:* One 1,030 h.p. Rolls-Royce Merlin II Vee type. *Span:* 54 ft. 0 in. (16.46 m.). *Length:* 42 ft. 1¾ in. (12.85 m.). *Height:* 15 ft. 6 in. (4.72 m.). *Normal take-off weight:* 10,792 lb. (4,895 kg.). *Maximum speed:* 257 m.p.h. (414 km./hr.) at 15,000 ft. (4,572 m.). *Operational ceiling:* 25,000 ft. (7,620 m.). *Maximum range:* 1,000 miles (1,609 km.). *Armament:* One 0.303 in. Browning machine-gun in starboard wing and one 0.303 in. Vickers K gun in rear of cabin; normal warload of four 250 lb. (113 kg.) bombs within the wings.

19

Junkers Ju 87B-1 of *Geschwader Stab/St. G. 2* "Immelmann", France, *ca.* summer 1940. *Engine:* One 900 h.p. Junkers Jumo 211A-1 inverted-Vee type. *Span:* 45 ft. 3¼ in. (13.80 m.). *Length:* 36 ft. 5 in. (11.10 m.). *Height:* 12 ft. 8½ in. (3.87 m.). *Normal take-off weight:* 9,370 lb. (4,250 kg.). *Maximum speed:* 242 m.p.h. (390 km./hr.) at 13,410 ft. (4,400 m.). *Operational ceiling:* 26,250 ft. (8,000 m.). *Range with 1,102 lb (500 kg.) bomb load:* 342 miles (550 km.). *Armament:* One 7.9 mm. MG 17 machine-gun in each wing and one 7.9 mm. MG 15 gun in rear of cabin; one 1,102 lb. (500 kg.) or 551 lb. (250 kg.) bomb beneath fuselage and up to four 110 lb. (50 kg.) bombs beneath the wings.

NAKAJIMA C6N (Japan)

20

Nakajima C6N1-1B Model 21 *Saiun* from the carrier *Zuikaku*, 1944. *Engine:* One 1,990 h.p. Nakajima Homare 21 radial. *Span:* 41 ft. 0⅛ in. (12.50 m.). *Length:* 36 ft. 5¾ in. (11.12 m.). *Height:* 12 ft. 11⅞ in. (3.96 m.). *Maximum take-off weight:* 11,596 lb. (5,260 kg.). *Maximum speed:* 395 m.p.h. (635 km./hr.) at 19,685 ft. (6,000 m.). *Operational ceiling:* 37,070 ft. (11,300 m.). *Maximum range:* 2,855 miles (4,595 km.). *Armament:* One 7.92 mm. machine-gun in rear of cabin.

21

Heinkel He 115B-1, ex works with factory flight test codes, 1939-40. *Engines:* Two 970 h.p. BMW 132K radials. *Span:* 73 ft. 1 in. (22.28 m.). *Length:* 56 ft. 9 in. (17.30 m.). *Height:* 21 ft. 7¾ in. (6.60 m.). *Maximum take-off weight:* 22,928 lb. (10,400 kg.). *Maximum speed:* 203 m.p.h. (327 km./hr.) at 11,155 ft. (3,400 m.). *Operational ceiling:* 17,060 ft. (5,200 m.). *Maximum range:* 2,082 miles (3,350 km.). *Armament:* Single 7.9 mm. MG 15 machine-guns in nose and dorsal positions; five 551 lb. (250 kg.) bombs, or two such bombs and one 1,764 lb. (800 kg.) torpedo or one 2,028 lb. (920 kg.) sea mine.

WELLINGTON (U.K.)

22

Vickers Wellington III of No. 419 Squadron RCAF, 1941-42. *Engines:* Two 1,500 h.p. Bristol Hercules XI radials. *Span:* 86 ft. 2 in. (26.26 m.). *Length:* 64 ft. 7 in. (19.68 m.). *Height:* 17 ft. 6 in. (5.33 m.). *Maximum take-off weight:* 29,500 lb. (13,381 kg.). *Maximum speed:* 255 m.p.h. (410 km./hr.) at 12,500 ft. (3,810 m.). *Operational ceiling:* 19,000 ft. (5,791 m.). *Range with 1,500 lb. (680 kg.) bomb load:* 2,200 miles (3,541 km.). *Armament:* Two 0.303 in. machine-guns in nose turret, four in tail turret and two in beam positions; up to 4,500 lb. (2,041 kg.) of bombs internally.

HEINKEL He 111 (Germany)

23

Heinkel He 111H-3 of III/KG.53 during the Battle of Britain, summer 1940.
Engines: Two 1,200 h.p. Junkers Jumo 211D-1 inverted-Vee type. *Span:* 74 ft.
1¾ in. (22.60 m.). *Length:* 53 ft. 9⅝ in. (16.40 m.). *Height:* 13 ft. 1½ in. (4.00 m.).
Normal take-off weight: 24,912 lb. (11,300 kg.). *Maximum speed:* 258 m.p.h.
(415 km./hr.) at 16,400 ft. (5,000 m.). *Operational ceiling:* 25,590 ft. (7,800 m.).
Range with maximum bomb load: 758 miles (1,220 km.). *Armament:* One 20
mm. MG FF cannon in ventral gondola, and five 7.9 mm. MG 15 machine-guns
in nose, dorsal, ventral and beam positions; up to 4,409 lb. (2,000 kg.) of bombs
internally.

39

ANSON (U.K.)

24

Avro Anson ASR I of No. 281 Squadron RAF, late 1943. *Engines:* Two 350 h.p. Armstrong Siddeley Cheetah IX radials. *Span:* 56 ft. 6 in. (17.22 m.). *Length:* 42 ft. 3 in. (12.88 m.). *Height:* 13 ft. 1 in. (3.99 m.). *Maximum take-off weight:* 8,000 lb. (3,629 kg.). *Maximum speed:* 188 m.p.h. (303 km./hr.) at 7,000 ft. (2,134 m.). *Operational ceiling:* 19,000 ft. (5,791 m.). *Range:* 790 miles (1,271 km.). *Armament:* One 0.303 in. machine-gun on port side of front fuselage and one in dorsal turret.

25

Ilyushin Il-4 (DB-3F) of the VVS-VMF (Soviet Naval Aviation), Baltic Sea area, *ca.* 1941-42. *Engines:* Two 1,100 h.p. M-88B radials. *Span:* 70 ft. $4\frac{1}{8}$ in. (21.44 m.). *Length:* 48 ft. $6\frac{3}{8}$ in. (14.80 m.). *Height:* approximately 13 ft. 9 in. (4.20 m.). *Maximum take-off weight:* 22,046 lb. (10,000 kg.). *Maximum speed:* 255 m.p.h. (410 km./hr.) at 21,000 ft. (6,400 m.). *Operational ceiling:* 29,530 ft. (9,000 m.). *Maximum range with 2,205 lb. (1,000 kg.) bomb load:* 2,647 miles (4,260 km.). *Armament:* Three 7.62 mm. ShKAS or 12.7 mm. BS machine-guns, one each in nose, dorsal and ventral positions; 2,205 lb. (1,000 kg.) of bombs internally, plus one 2,072 lb. (940 kg.) 45-36-AN or -AV torpedo or up to 3,307 lb. (1,500 kg.) of bombs beneath the fuselage.

MARTIN 167 (U.S.A.)

26

Martin 167A-3 (Model 167F) of the *Armée de l'Air* (unit unknown), France, *ca.* March/April 1940. *Engines:* Two 1,050 h.p. Pratt & Whitney R-1830-S1C3-G Twin Wasp radials. *Span:* 61 ft. 4 in. (18.69 m.). *Length:* 46 ft. 8 in. (14.22 m.). *Height:* 10 ft. 1 in. (3.07 m.). *Normal take-off weight:* 15,297 lb. (6,939 kg.). *Maximum speed:* 304 m.p.h. (489 km./hr.) at 14,000 ft. (4,267 m.). *Operational ceiling:* 29,500 ft. (8,992 m.). *Maximum range:* 1,300 miles (2,092 km.). *Armament:* Two 0.30 in. machine-guns in each wing and one each in dorsal and ventral positions; up to 1,250 lb. (567 kg.) of bombs internally.

27

Rootes-built Blenheim IVL of No. 13 OTU, RAF, fitted with leading-edge balloon-cable cutters, *ca.* August 1942. *Engines:* Two 920 h.p. Bristol Mercury XV radials. *Span:* 56 ft. 4 in. (17.17 m.). *Length:* 42 ft. 9 in. (13.04 m.). *Height:* 12 ft. 10 in. (3.91 m.). *Maximum take-off weight:* 14,400 lb. (6,531 kg.). *Maximum speed:* 266 m.p.h. (428 km./hr.) at 11,800 ft. (3,597 m.). *Operational ceiling:* 27,000 ft. (8,230 m.). *Maximum range:* 1,950 miles (3,138 km.). *Armament:* One 0.303 in. Vickers K gun in nose, two 0.303 in. Browning machine-guns in dorsal turret and two in fairing beneath nose; up to 1,000 lb. (454 kg.) of bombs internally.

BEAUFIGHTER (U.K.)

28

Bristol Beaufighter TF VIC of Coastal Command Development Unit, RAF *ca.* March/April 1943. *Engines:* Two 1,670 h.p. Bristol Hercules VI or XVI radials. *Span:* 57 ft. 10 in. (17.63 m.). *Length:* 41 ft. 4 in. (12.60 m.). *Height:* 15 ft. 10 in. (4.83 m.). *Maximum take-off weight:* 23,884 lb. (10,834 kg.). *Maximum speed:* 312 m.p.h. (502 km./hr.) at 14,000 ft. (4,267 m.). *Operational ceiling:* 26,000 ft. (7,925 m.). *Normal range:* 1,540 miles (2,478 km.). *Armament:* Four 20 mm. Hispano cannon in nose, three 0.303 in. Browning machine-guns in each wing, and one 0.303 in. Vickers K gun in dorsal position; one 1,605 lb. (728 kg.). torpedo beneath fuselage.

BEAUFORT (U.K.)

29

Bristol Beaufort I of No. 42 Squadron RAF, March 1941. *Engines:* Two 1,130 h.p.
Bristol Taurus VI radials. *Span:* 57 ft. 10 in. (17.63 m.). *Length:* 44 ft. 2 in.
(13.46 m.). *Height:* 14 ft. 3 in. (4.34 m.). *Maximum take-off weight:* 21,228 lb.
(9,628 kg.). *Maximum speed (with torpedo):* 225 m.p.h. (362 km./hr.) at 5,000
ft. (1,524 m.). *Operational ceiling:* 16,500 ft. (5,029 m.). *Maximum range:*
1,600 miles (2,575 km.). *Armament:* Two 0.303 in. Vickers K guns in dorsal
turret and one in port wing, plus one 0.303 in. rear-firing Browning machine-
gun beneath nose; up to 1,000 lb. (454 kg.) of bombs internally and 500 lb.
(227 kg.) externally, or one 1,605 lb. (728 kg.) torpedo semi-internally.

MOSQUITO (U.K.)

30

De Havilland Mosquito B XVI of No. 571 (Pathfinder) Squadron RAF, spring 1944. *Engines:* Two 1,680 h.p. Rolls-Royce Merlin 72 or 76 Vee type. *Span:* 54 ft. 2 in. (16.51 m.). *Length:* 40 ft. 6 in. (12.34 m.). *Height:* 15 ft. 3½ in. (4.66 m.). *Normal take-off weight:* 19,093 lb. (8,660 kg.). *Maximum speed:* 408 m.p.h. (656 km./hr.) at 26,000 ft. (7,925 m.). *Operational ceiling:* 37,000 ft. (11,278 m.). *Range with maximum bomb load:* 1,370 miles (2,205 km.). *Armament:* No guns; maximum bomb load of 4,000 lb. (1,814 kg.).

JUNKERS Ju 88 (Germany)

31

Junkers Ju 88A-4/Trop. of 2(F)/123, Western Desert, summer 1942. *Engines:* Two 1,340 h.p. Junkers Jumo 211J inverted-Vee type. *Span:* 65 ft. 7⅜ in. (20.00 m.). *Length:* 47 ft. 2⅞ in. (14.40 m.). *Height:* 15 ft. 11 in. (4.85 m.). *Maximum take-off weight:* 30,865 lb. (14,000 kg.). *Maximum speed:* 269 m.p.h. (433 km./hr.) at 14,765 ft. (4,500 m.). *Operational ceiling:* 26,900 ft. (8,200 m.). *Normal range:* 1,112 miles (1,790 km.). *Typical armament:* Nine 7.9 mm. MG 81 machine-guns, two in extreme nose, one in front of pilot, two in rear of cabin, and two forward and two aft in under-nose cupola; 1,102 lb. (500 kg.) of bombs internally and up to 2,205 lb. (1,000 kg.) externally.

47

BOSTON (U.S.A.)

32

Douglas Boston IIIA of No. 342 (Lorraine) Squadron FAFL, summer 1944.
Engines: Two 1,600 h.p. Wright R-2600-23 Cyclone radials. *Span:* 61 ft. 4 in.
(18.69 m.). *Length:* 47 ft. 3 in. (14.40 m.). *Height:* 17 ft. 7 in. (5.36 m.).
Maximum take-off weight: 24,500 lb. (11,113 kg.). *Maximum speed:* 342 m.p.h.
(550 km./hr.) at 13,000 ft. (3,962 m.). *Operational ceiling:* 24,250 ft. (7,391 m.).
Range with maximum bomb load: 1,050 miles (1,690 km.). *Armament:* Two
0.303 in. Browning machine-guns on each side of nose, and two in dorsal
position, plus one 0.303 in. Vickers K gun in ventral position; up to 2,000 lb.
(907 kg.) of bombs internally.

33

Douglas A-26B Invader of the US Ninth Air Force, ETO 1944-45. *Engines:* Two 2,000 h.p. Pratt & Whitney R-2800-27 or -71 Double Wasp radials. *Span:* 70 ft. 0 in. (21.34 m.). *Length:* 50 ft. 0 in. (15.24 m.). *Height:* 18 ft. 6 in. (5.64 m.). *Maximum take-off weight:* 35,000 lb. (15,876 kg.). *Maximum speed:* 355 m.p.h. (571 km./hr.) at 15,000 ft. (4,572 m.). *Operational ceiling:* 22,100 ft. (6,736 m.). *Range with maximum bomb load:* 1,400 miles (2,253 km.). *Armament:* Ten 0.50 in. machine-guns, six in nose and two each in dorsal and ventral turrets; up to 4,000 lb. (1,814 kg.) of bombs internally.

BALTIMORE (U.S.A.)

34

Martin Baltimore IV, ex-RAF machine seconded to the *Stormo Baltimore* of the Italian Co-Belligerent Air Force, *ca.* November 1944. *Engines:* Two 1,660 h.p. Wright R-2600-19 Double-Row Cyclone radials. *Span:* 61 ft. 4 in. (18.69 m.). *Length:* 48 ft. 6 in. (14.78 m.). *Height:* 17 ft. 9 in. (5.41 m.). *Maximum take-off weight:* 23,000 lb. (10,433 kg.). *Maximum speed:* 302 m.p.h. (486 km./hr.) at 11,000 ft. (3,353 m.). *Operational ceiling:* 24,000 ft. (7,315 m.). *Range with 1,000 lb. (454 kg.) bomb load:* 1,082 miles (1,741 km.). *Armament:* Two 0.50 in. machine-guns in dorsal turret, two 0.303 in. machine-guns in each wing and up to six 0.30 in. machine-guns in ventral positions; up to 2,000 lb. (907 kg.) of bombs internally.

35

Martin B-26B-55 Marauder of the 598th Bomber Squadron, 397th Bomber Group, US Ninth Air Force, June 1944. Engines: Two 1,920 h.p. Pratt & Whitney R-2800-43 Double Wasp radials. *Span:* 71 ft. 0 in. (21.64 m.). *Length:* 58 ft. 3 in. (17.75 m.). *Height:* 21 ft. 6 in. (6.55 m.). *Maximum take-off weight:* 37,000 lb. (16,783 kg.). *Maximum speed:* 282 m.p.h. (454 km./hr.) at 15,000 ft. (4,572 m.). *Operational ceiling:* 21,700 ft. (6,614 m.). *Range with 3,000 lb. (1,361 kg.) bomb load:* 1,150 miles (1,851 km.). *Armament:* Eleven 0.50 in. machine-guns, in dorsal and tail turrets (two each), beam positions (one each), nose (one) and external nose blisters (two each side), plus one 0.30 in. gun in extreme nose; up to 5,200 lb. (2,359 kg.) of bombs.

PZL P.37 (Poland)

36

PZL P.37 Łoś B, possibly an aircraft of *Dyon* X/I, 1st Air Regiment, Warsaw 1939. *Engines:* Two 918 h.p. PZL-built Bristol Pegasus XX radials. *Span:* 58 ft. 8¾ in. (17.90 m.). *Length:* 42 ft. 3⅞ in. (12.90 m.). *Height:* 16 ft. 8 in. (5.08 m.). *Normal take-off weight:* 18,739 lb. (8,500 kg.). *Maximum speed:* 273 m.p.h. (440 km./hr.) at 12,140 ft. (3,700 m.). *Operational ceiling:* 19,685 ft. (6,000 m.). *Range with 3,880 lb. (1,760 kg.) bomb load:* 1,616 miles (2,600 km.). *Armament:* Single 7.7 mm. KM Wz.37 machine-guns in each of nose, dorsal and ventral positions; normal warload of twenty 243 lb. (110 kg.) bombs in wing centre-section; maximum permissible load of 5,688 lb. (2,580 kg.).

37

Mitsubishi Ki-21-IIb Model 2B of the 1st Squadron, 14th Group JAAF, Philippines, 1944. *Engines:* Two 1,500 h.p. Mitsubishi Ha-101 radials. *Span:* 73 ft. 9$\frac{7}{8}$ in. (22.50 m.). *Length:* 52 ft. 6 in. (16.00 m.). *Height:* 15 ft. 11 in. (4.85 m.). *Normal take-off weight:* 21,407 lb. (9,710 kg.). *Maximum speed:* 302 m.p.h. (486 km./hr.) at 15,485 ft. (4,720 m.). *Operational ceiling:* 32,810 ft. (10,000 m.). *Normal range:* 1,678 miles (2,700 km.). *Armament:* One 12.7 mm. Type 1 machine-gun in dorsal turret, five 7.7 mm. Type 89 machine-guns (one each in nose, tail, ventral and two beam positions); up to 2,205 lb. (1,000 kg.) of bombs internally.

MITSUBISHI G4M (Japan)

38

Mitsubishi G4M2a Model 24 of the 753rd Air Corps JNAF, Philippines, autumn 1944. *Engines:* Two 1,850 h.p. Mitsubishi Kasei 25 radials. *Span:* 81 ft. 7$\frac{7}{8}$ in. (24.89 m.). *Length:* 64 ft. 4$\frac{7}{8}$ in. (19.63 m.). *Height:* 13 ft. 5$\frac{7}{8}$ in. (4.11 m.). *Maximum take-off weight:* 33,069 lb. (15,000 kg.). *Maximum speed:* 272 m.p.h. (437 km./hr.) at 15,090 ft. (4,600 m.). *Operational ceiling:* 29,365 ft. (8,950 m.). *Normal range:* 1,497 miles (2,410 km.). *Armament:* Four 20 mm. Type 99 cannon (one each in dorsal, tail and two beam positions), and one 7.7 mm. Type 97 machine-gun in nose; up to 2,205 lb. (1,000 kg.) of bombs internally or one 1,764 lb. (800 kg.) torpedo.

39

Mitsubishi Ki-67-lb Model 1B *Hiryu* of the JAAF (unit unidentified), 1945.
Engines: Two 1,900 h.p. Mitsubishi Ha-104 radials. *Span:* 73 ft. $9\frac{7}{8}$ in. (22.50 m.).
Length: 61 ft. $4\frac{1}{4}$ in. (18.70 m.). *Height:* 18 ft. $4\frac{1}{2}$ in. (5.60 m.). *Normal take-off
weight:* 30,346 lb. (13,765 kg.). *Maximum speed:* 334 m.p.h. (537 km./hr.) at
19,980 ft. (6,090 m.). *Operational ceiling:* 31,070 ft. (9,470 m.). *Normal range:*
1,740 miles (2,800 km.). *Armament:* One 20 mm. Ho-5 cannon in dorsal turret,
four 12.7 mm. Type 1 machine-guns (one each in nose, tail and two beam
positions); up to 1,764 lb. (800 kg.) of bombs internally.

NAKAJIMA Ki-49 (Japan)

40

Nakajima Ki-49-IIa Model 2A *Donryu* of the 3rd Squadron, 95th Group JAAF, 1944-45. *Engines:* Two 1,450 h.p. Nakajima Ha-109-II radials. *Span:* 66 ft. 7¼ in. (20.30 m.). *Length:* 53 ft. 1¾ in. (16.20 m.). *Height:* 13 ft. 11⅜ in. (4.25 m.). *Normal take-off weight:* 23,545 lb. (10,680 kg.). *Maximum speed:* 304 m.p.h. (490 km./hr.) at 16,405 ft. (5,000 m.). *Operational ceiling:* 26,770 ft. (8,160 m.). *Normal range:* 1,491 miles (2,400 km.). *Armament:* One 20 mm. cannon in dorsal turret, and five 7.92 mm. machine-guns in nose, tail, ventral and beam positions; up to 2,205 lb. (1,000 kg.) of bombs internally.

MITSUBISHI Ki-46 (Japan)

41
Mitsubishi Ki-46-III Model 3 of the 2nd Squadron, 81st Group JAAF, Burma 1944. *Engines:* Two 1,500 h.p. Mitsubishi Ha-112-II radials. *Span:* 48 ft. 2¾ in. (14.70 m.). *Length:* 36 ft. 1 in. (11.00 m.). *Height:* 12 ft. 8¾ in. (3.88 m.). *Maximum take-off weight:* 14,330 lb. (6,500 kg.). *Maximum speed:* 391 m.p.h. (630 km./hr.) at 19,685 ft. (6,000 m.). *Operational ceiling:* 34,450 ft. (10,500 m.). *Maximum range:* 2,485 miles (4,000 km.). *Armament:* None.

YOKOSUKA P1Y (Japan)

42

Yokosuka P1Y1 Model 11 *Ginga* of No. 262 Bomber Squadron, 762nd Air Corps JNAF, 1944-45. *Engines:* Two 1,820 h.p. Nakajima Homare 11 radials. *Span:* 65 ft. 7⅜ in. (20.00 m.). *Length:* 49 ft. 2½ in. (15.00 m.). *Height:* 14 ft. 1¼ in. (4.30 m.). *Maximum take-off weight:* 29,762 lb. (13,500 kg.). *Maximum speed:* 345 m.p.h. (556 km./hr.) at 19,360 ft. (5,900 m.). *Operational ceiling:* 33,530 ft. (10,220 m.). *Range:* 2,728 miles (4,390 km.). *Armament:* One 20 mm. cannon in nose, one 12.7 mm. machine-gun in dorsal position; up to 1,102 lb. (500 kg.). of bombs internally, and further small bombs, or one 1,874 lb. (850 kg.). or 1,764 lb. (800 kg.) torpedo, externally.

43

Heinkel He 177A-5/R7 *Greif* of *Staffel* 6, II/KG.40, Bordeaux-Mérignac, *ca.* November 1943. *Engines:* Two 2,950 h.p. Daimler-Benz DB 610 (coupled DB 605) radials. *Span:* 103 ft. 1¾ in. (31.44 m.). *Length:* 72 ft. 2⅛ in. (22.00 m.). *Height:* 21 ft. 0 in. (6.40 m.). *Normal take-off weight:* 59,966 lb. (27,200 kg.). *Maximum speed:* 303 m.p.h. (488 km./hr.) at 20,010 ft. (6,100 m.). *Operational ceiling:* 49,870 ft. (15,200 m.). *Maximum range with two Hs 293 missiles:* 3,107 miles (5,000 km.). *Armament:* One 20 mm. MG 151 cannon in front of under-nose cupola and one in tail; two 13 mm. MG 131 machine-guns in forward dorsal barbette and one in rear dorsal turret; and one 7.9 mm. MG 81 gun in nose and two in rear of under-nose cupola; up to 2,205 lb. (1,000 kg.) of bombs internally and two mines, torpedos or missiles externally.

CURTISS C-46 (U.S.A.)

44

Curtiss CW-20 *St. Louis* (prototype for C-46 series), as delivered for operation by BOAC, December 1941. *Engines:* Two 1,700 h.p. Wright 586-C14-BA2 Double-Row Cyclone radials. *Span:* 108 ft. 1 in. (32.94 m.). *Length:* 76 ft. 4 in. (23.27 m.). *Height:* 21 ft. 9 in. (6.63 m.). *Maximum take-off weight:* 45,000 lb. (20,412 kg.). *Maximum speed:* 240 m.p.h. (386 km./hr.) at sea level. *Operational ceiling:* 26,900 ft. (8,199 m.). *Normal range with 4,621 lb. (2,096 kg.) payload:* 2,000 miles (3,219 km.). *Armament:* None.

45

Douglas C-53C Skytrooper of the USAAF, El Kabrit, spring 1943. *Engines:* Two 1,200 h.p. Pratt & Whitney R-1830-92 Twin Wasp radials. *Span:* 95 ft. 0 in. (28.96 m.). *Length:* 64 ft. 5½ in. (19.65 m.). *Height:* 16 ft. 11 in. (5.16 m.). *Maximum take-off weight:* 29,300 lb, (13,290 kg.). *Maximum speed:* 210 m.p.h. (338 km./hr.) at 8,800 ft. (2,682 m.). *Operational ceiling:* 24,100 ft. (7,346 m.). *Normal range:* 1,350 miles (2,173 km.). *Armament:* None.

46

Consolidated Catalina I (PBY-5) of No. 209 Squadron RAF which spotted the *Bismarck* on 26 May 1941. *Engines:* Two 1,200 h.p. Pratt & Whitney R-1830-S1C3-G Twin Wasp radials. *Span:* 104 ft. 0 in. (31.70 m.). *Length:* 63 ft. 10½ in. (19.47 m.). *Height:* 18 ft. 10⅝ in. (5.76 m.). *Normal take-off weight:* 27,080 lb. (12,283 kg.). *Maximum speed:* 190 m.p.h. (306 km./hr.) at 10,500 ft. (3,200 m.). *Operational ceiling:* 24,000 ft. (7,315 m.). *Maximum range:* 4,000 miles (6,437 km.). *Armament:* Six 0.303 in. Vickers guns, one in bow, two in each side blister and one in ventral tunnel aft of hull step; up to 2,000 lb. (907 kg.) of bombs.

47

Saab-18A (B 18A) of F 11 Wing (3rd Division), *Kungl. Svenska Flygvapnet,*
1944-45. *Engines:* Two 1,065 h.p. SFA-built Pratt & Whitney R-1830-S1C3-G
Twin Wasp radials. *Span:* 55 ft. $9\frac{1}{4}$ in. (17.00 m.). *Length:* 43 ft. $4\frac{7}{8}$ in. (13.23 m.).
Height: 14 ft. $3\frac{1}{4}$ in. (4.35 m.). *Normal take-off weight:* 17,946 lb. (8,140 kg.).
Maximum speed: 289 m.p.h. (465 km./hr.) at 19,685 ft. (6,000 m.). *Operational
ceiling:* 26,250 ft. (8,000 m.). *Maximum range:* 1,367 miles (2,200 km.).
Armament: One 13.2 mm. machine-gun in rear of crew cabin and one in rear of
under-nose fairing, and one 7.9 mm. gun in starboard side of nose; up to 3,307 lb.
(1,500 kg.) of bombs.

DORNIER Do 217 (Germany)

48

Dornier Do 217E-2 of 5/KG.6, France, early 1943. *Engines:* Two 1,580 h.p. BMW 801M radials. *Span:* 62 ft. 4 in. (19.00 m.). *Length:* 56 ft 9⅛ in. (17.30 m.). *Height:* 16 ft. 4⅞ in. (5.00 m.). *Normal take-off weight:* 33,069 lb. (15,000 kg.). *Maximum speed:* 320 m.p.h. (515 km./hr.) at 17,060 ft. (5,200 m.). *Operational ceiling:* 24,610 ft. (7,500 m.). *Maximum range:* 1,429 miles (2,300 km.). *Armament:* One 15 mm. MG 151 cannon in nose, one 13 mm. MG 131 machine-gun in dorsal turret and one in rear of under-nose cupola, one 7.9 mm. MG 15 gun in nose and one each side in rear of cabin; up to 5,512 lb. (2,500 kg.) of bombs internally and 3,307 lb. (1,500 kg.) externally.

64

DORNIER Do 17 (Germany)

49

Dornier Do 17Z-2 of 15/KG.53 (*Kroaten*), Eastern Front, September 1942. *Engines:* Two 1,000 h.p. Bramo Fafnir 323P radials. *Span:* 59 ft. 0⅝ in. (18.00 m.). *Length:* 51 ft. 9⅜ in. (15.79 m.). *Height:* 14 ft. 11½ in. (4.56 m.). *Normal take-off weight:* 18,872 lb. (8,560 kg.). *Maximum speed:* 224 m.p.h. (360 km./hr.) at 13,120 ft. (4,000 m.). *Operational ceiling:* 22,965 ft. (7,000 m.). *Maximum range with 1,102 lb. (500 kg.) bomb load and auxiliary fuel:* 721 miles (1,160 km.). *Armament:* Six 7.9 mm. MG 15 machine-guns: one in nose, one in front of cabin, one each side in rear of cabin, one aft of cabin and one in ventral position; up to 2,205 lb. (1,000 kg.) of bombs internally.

65

WHITLEY (U.K.)

50

Armstrong Whitworth Whitley V of No. 77 Squadron RAF, April 1940. *Engines:* Two 1,075 h.p. Rolls-Royce Merlin X Vee type. *Span:* 84 ft. 0 in. (25.60 m.). *Length:* 70 ft. 6 in. (21.49 m.). *Height:* 15 ft. 0 in. (4.57 m.). *Normal take-off weight:* 33,500 lb. (15,196 kg.). *Maximum speed:* 230 m.p.h. (370 km./hr.) at 16,400 ft. (5,000 m.). *Operational ceiling:* 26,000 ft. (7,925 m.). *Maximum range:* 2,400 miles (3,862 km.). *Armament:* One 0.303 in. Vickers gun in nose turret and four 0.303 in. Browning machine-guns in tail turret; up to 7,000 lb. (3,175 kg.) of bombs internally.

51

Handley Page Hampden I of No. 44 (Rhodesia) Squadron RAF, summer 1941. *Engines:* Two 980 h.p. Bristol Pegasus XVIII radials. *Span:* 69 ft. 2 in. (21.08 m.). *Length:* 53 ft. 7 in. (16.33 m.). *Height:* 14 ft. 4 in. (4.37 m.). *Normal take-off weight:* 18,756 lb. (8,508 kg.). *Maximum speed:* 265 m.p.h. (426 km./hr.) at 15,500 ft. (4,724 m.). *Operational ceiling:* 22,700 ft. (6,919 m.). *Range with maximum bomb load:* 1,095 miles (1,762 km.). *Armament:* Six 0.303 in. Vickers K guns (two in nose and two each in dorsal and ventral positions); up to 4,000 lb. (1,814 kg.) of bombs internally.

FIAT B.R.20 (Italy)

52

Fiat B.R.20M *Cicogna* of the 4° *Squadriglia*, 11° *Gruppo*, 13° *Stormo B.T.*, northern Italy, autumn 1940. *Engines:* Two 1,000 h.p. Fiat A.80 RC 41 radials. *Span:* 70 ft. 8⅞ in. (21.56 m.). *Length:* 55 ft. 0¾ in. (16.78 m.). *Height:* 15 ft. 7 in. (4.75 m.). *Normal take-off weight:* 23,038 lb. (10,450 kg.). *Maximum speed:* 267 m.p.h. (430 km./hr.) at 13,120 ft. (4,000 m.). *Operational ceiling:* 22,145 ft. (6,750 m.). *Range:* 1,243 miles (2,000 km.). *Armament:* One 12.7 mm. Breda-SAFAT machine-gun in dorsal turret and three 7.7 mm. Breda-SAFAT guns (one each in nose, tail and ventral positions); up to 3,527 lb. (1,600 kg.) of bombs internally.

53

North American B-25A of the 34th Bomber Squadron, 17th Bombardment Group USAAC, summer 1941. *Engines:* Two 1,700 h.p. Wright R-2600-9 Cyclone radials. *Span:* 67 ft. 7 in. (20.60 m.). *Length:* 54 ft. 1 in. (16.48 m.). *Height:* 15 ft. 9 in. (4.80 m.). *Maximum take-off weight:* 27,100 lb. (12,292 kg.). *Maximum speed:* 315 m.p.h. (507 km./hr.) at 15,000 ft. (4,572 m.). *Operational ceiling:* 27,000 ft. (8,230 m.). *Range with maximum bomb load:* 1,350 miles (2,173 km.). *Armament:* One 0.50 in. machine-gun in tail, and three 0.30 in. guns (one in nose and one in each beam position); up to 3,000 lb. (1,361 kg.) of bombs internally.

HUDSON (U.S.A.)

54

Lockheed Hudson III of No. 269 Squadron RAF, winter 1941-42. *Engines:* Two 1,200 h.p. Wright GR-1820-G205A Cyclone radials. *Span:* 65 ft. 6 in. (19.96 m.). *Length:* 44 ft. 4 in. (13.51 m.). *Height:* 11 ft. 10½ in. (3.62 m.). *Maximum take-off weight:* 20,000 lb. (9,072 kg.). *Maximum speed:* 255 m.p.h. (410 km./hr.) at 5,000 ft. (1,524 m.). *Operational ceiling:* 24,500 ft. (7,468 m.). *Maximum range:* 2,160 miles (3,476 km.). *Armament:* Seven 0.303 in. machine-guns (two each in nose and dorsal turret, one in each beam position, and one in ventral position); up to 750 lb. (340 kg.) of bombs.

55

Lockheed Ventura I of No. 21 Squadron RAF, summer/autumn 1942. *Engines:* Two 2,000 h.p. Pratt & Whitney GR-2800-S1A4-G Double Wasp radials. *Span:* 65 ft. 6 in. (19.96 m.). *Length:* 51 ft. 5 in. (15.67 m.). *Height:* 11 ft. 10½ in. (3.62 m.). *Maximum take-off weight:* 26,000 lb. (11,793 kg.). *Maximum speed:* 312 m.p.h. (502 km./hr.) at 6,800 ft. (2,073 m.). *Operational ceiling:* 25,200 ft. (7,681 m.). *Range with maximum bomb load:* 1,000 miles (1,609 km.). *Armament:* Two 0.50 in. machine-guns in nose, six 0.303 in. machine-guns (two each in nose, dorsal turret and ventral position); up to 2,500 lb. (1,134 kg.) of bombs internally.

71

LODESTAR (U.S.A.)

56

Lockheed C-60A Lodestar of the USAAF, 1943-44. *Engines:* Two 1,200 h.p. Wright R-1820-87 Cyclone radials. *Span:* 65 ft. 6 in. (19.96 m.). *Length:* 49 ft. 9⅞ in. (15.19 m.). *Height:* 11 ft. 10½ in. (3.62 m.). *Normal take-off weight:* 18,500 lb. (8,392 kg.). *Maximum speed:* 266 m.p.h. (428 km./hr.) at 17,000 ft. (5,182 m.). *Operational ceiling:* 27,000 ft. (8,230 m.). *Maximum range with full load:* 1,660 miles (2,672 km.). *Armament:* None.

ALBEMARLE (U.K.)

57

Armstrong Whitworth Albemarle ST I of No. 297 Squadron RAF, June 1944.
Engines: Two 1,590 h.p. Bristol Hercules XI radials. *Span:* 77 ft. 0 in. (23.47 m.).
Length: 59 ft. 11 in. (18.26 m.). *Height:* 15 ft. 7 in. (4.75 m.). *Maximum take-off
weight:* 36,500 lb. (16,556 kg.). *Maximum speed:* 265 m.p.h. (426 km./hr.) at
10,500 ft. (3,200 m.). *Operational ceiling:* 18,000 ft. (5,486 m.). *Normal range:*
1,300 miles (2,092 km.). *Armament:* Four 0.303 in. machine-guns in dorsal
turret.

EXPEDITER (U.S.A.)

58

Beech Expediter II (UC-45F) of the Royal Navy, personal transport of Vice-Admiral Sir Dennis Boyd, 1945. *Engines:* Two 450 h.p. Pratt & Whitney R-985-AN-1 Wasp Junior radials. *Span:* 47 ft. 7¾ in. (14.52 m.). *Length:* 34 ft. 2¾ in (10.43 m.). *Height:* 9 ft. 4 in. (2.84 m.). *Normal take-off weight:* 7,500 lb. (3,402 kg.). *Maximum speed:* 223 m.p.h. (359 km./hr.) at sea level. *Operational ceiling:* 27,000 ft. (8,230 m.). *Maximum range:* 1,200 miles (1,931 km.). *Armament:* None.

FOCKE-WULF Fw 189 (Germany)

59

Focke-Wulf Fw 189A-2 of 1(H)/32 serving with *Luftflotte* 5, Eastern Front (White Sea area) October 1942. *Engines:* Two 465 h.p. Argus As 410A-1 inverted-Vee type. *Span:* 60 ft. 4⅜ in. (18.40 m.). *Length:* 39 ft. 4½ in. (12.00 m.). *Height:* 10 ft. 2 in. (3.10 m.). *Normal take-off weight:* 8,708 lb. (3,950 kg.). *Maximum speed:* 217 m.p.h. (350 km./hr.) at 7,870 ft. (2,400 m.). *Operational ceiling:* 23,950 ft. (7,300 m.). *Normal range:* 416 miles (670 km.). *Armament:* Four 7.9 mm. MG 81 machine-guns (two in dorsal position and two in rear of nacelle), and one 7.9 mm. MG 17 gun in each wing root; four 110 lb. (50 kg.) bombs beneath the wings.

BLOHM und VOSS Bv 138 (Germany)

60

Blohm und Voss Bv 138C-1 of an unidentified *Aufklärungsgruppe* (Reconnaissance Group), possibly in the Baltic Sea area, *ca.* 1942-43. *Engines:* Three 880 h.p. Junkers Jumo 205D vertically-opposed diesel type. *Span:* 88 ft. 7 in. (27.00 m.). *Length:* 65 ft. 1½ in. (19.85 m.). *Height:* 19 ft. 4¼ in. (5.90 m.). *Normal take-off weight:* 31,967 lb. (14,500 kg.). *Maximum speed:* 171 m.p.h. (275 km./hr.) at 6,560 ft. (2,000 m.). *Operational ceiling:* 16,400 ft. (5,000 m.). *Maximum range:* 2,760 miles (4,355 km.). *Armament:* Two 20 mm. MG 151 cannon (one each in bow and rear turrets), one 13 mm. MG 131 machine-gun aft of central engine, and provision for one 7.9 mm. MG 15 gun in starboard side of hull; three or six 110 lb. (50 kg.) bombs or four 331 lb. (150 kg.) depth charges beneath starboard centre-section.

61

C.R.D.A. Cant. Z.506B *Airone* Serie XII, formerly of the 139° *Squadriglia da Ricognizione Marittima,* in the insignia of the Italian Co-Belligerent Air Force, 1943–44. *Engines:* Three 750 h.p. Alfa Romeo 126 RC 34 radials. *Span:* 86 ft. 11¼ in. (26.50 m.). *Length:* 63 ft. 1⅞ in. (19.25 m.). *Height:* 24 ft. 5⅜ in. (7.45 m.). *Maximum take-off weight:* 28,008 lb. (12,705 kg.). *Maximum speed:* 217 m.p.h. (350 km./hr.) at 13,120 ft. (4,000 m.). *Operational ceiling:* 24,000 ft. (7,320 m.). *Range with 2,094 lb. (950 kg.) bomb load:* 1,243 miles (2,000 km.). *Armament:* One 12.7 mm. Scotti machine-gun in dorsal turret, one 7.7 mm. Breda-SAFAT machine-gun in ventral position and one in each beam position; up to 2,645 lb. (1,200 kg.) of bombs.

JUNKERS Ju 52/3m (Germany)

62

Junkers Ju 52/3m of *Kampffliegerschüle* Thorn, winter 1942–43. *Engines:* Three 830 h.p. BMW 132T radials. *Span:* 95 ft. 11½ in. (29.25 m.). *Length:* 62 ft. 0 in. (18.90 m.). *Height:* 14 ft. 9⅛ in. (4.50 m.). *Maximum take-off weight:* 24,317 lb. (11,030 kg.). *Maximum speed:* 190 m.p.h. (305 km./hr.) at 8,200 ft. (2,500 m.). *Operational ceiling:* 18,045 ft. (5,500 m.). *Range with 2,205 lb.* (*1,000 kg.*) *payload:* 808 miles (1,300 km.). *Armament:* One 13 mm. MG 131 machine-gun in dorsal position and two 7.9 mm. MG 15 guns firing through passengers' windows.

CANT. Z.1007 (Italy)

63

C.R.D.A. Cant. Z.1007*bis Alcione* of the 211° *Squadriglia B.T.,* Mediterranean area 1941–42. *Engines:* Three 1,000 h.p. Piaggio P.XI*bis* RC 40 radials. *Span:* 81 ft. 4⅜ in. (24.80 m.). *Length:* 60 ft. 2⅜ in. (18.35 m.). *Height:* 17 ft. 1½ in. (5.22 m.). *Maximum take-off weight:* 30,029 lb. (13,621 kg.). *Maximum speed:* 283 m.p.h. (455 km./hr.) at 17,220 ft. (5,250 m.). *Operational ceiling:* 24,610 ft. (7,500 m.). *Range with maximum bomb load:* 1,367 miles (2,200 km.). *Armament:* One 12.7 mm. Breda-SAFAT machine-gun in dorsal turret, one in ventral position and one 7.7 mm. gun in each beam position; up to 4,409 lb. (2,000 kg.) of bombs internally.

SAVOIA-MARCHETTI S.M.79 (Italy)

64

Savoia-Marchetti S.M.79-II *Sparviero* of the 59° *Squadriglia*, 33° *Gruppo*, 11° *Stormo B.T.*, Cyrenaica November 1940. *Engines:* Three 1,000 h.p. Piaggio P.XI RC 40 radials. *Span:* 69 ft. 6⅝ in. (21.20 m.). *Length:* 53 ft. 1¾ in. (16.20 m.). *Height:* 15 ft. 11 in. (4.60 m.). *Normal take-off weight:* 25,133 lb. (11,400 kg.). *Maximum speed:* 295 m.p.h. (475 km./hr.) at 13,120 ft. (4,000 m.). *Operational ceiling:* 27,890 ft. (8,500 m.). *Range with maximum bomb load:* 1,243 miles 2,000 km.). *Armament:* Three 12.7 mm. Breda-SAFAT machine-guns (one above pilot's cabin, one in dorsal position, one in ventral gondola), and one 7.7 mm. Lewis gun amidships to fire to port or starboard; up to 2,756 lb. (1,250 kg.) of bombs internally.

PETLYAKOV Pe-8 (U.S.S.R.)

65

Petlyakov Pe-8 of the Soviet Air Force, used for communications between Moscow and the UK, 1942. *Engines:* Four 1,350 h.p. Mikulin AM-35A Vee type. *Span:* 131 ft. 0⅜ in. (39.94 m.). *Length:* 73 ft. 8⅝ in. (22.47 m.). *Height:* 20 ft. 0⅛ in. (6.10 m.). *Maximum take-off weight:* 73,469 lb. (33,325 kg.). *Maximum speed:* 272 m.p.h. (438 km./hr.) at 24,935 ft. (7,600 m.). *Operational ceiling:* 31,988 ft. (9,750 m.). *Maximum range with 4,409 lb. (2,000 kg.) bomb load:* 3,383 miles (5,445 km.). *Armament:* One 20 mm. ShVAK cannon in each of the dorsal and tail turrets, one 12.7 mm. Beresin machine-gun in the rear of each inboard engine nacelle, and two 7.62 mm. ShKAS guns in nose turret; up to 8,818 lb. (4,000 kg.) of bombs internally.

STIRLING (U.K.)

66

Short Stirling B III of No. 199 Bomber Support Squadron RAF, autumn 1944. *Engines:* Four 1,650 h.p. Bristol Hercules XVI radials. *Span:* 99 ft. 1 in. (30.20 m.). *Length:* 87 ft. 3 in. (26.59 m.). *Height:* 22 ft. 9 in. (6.93 m.). *Maximum take-off weight:* 70,000 lb. (31,751 kg.). *Maximum speed:* 270 m.p.h. (435 km./hr.) at 14,500 ft. (4,420 m.). *Operational ceiling:* 17,000 ft. (5,182 m.). *Range with 3,500 lb.* (*1,588 kg.*) *bomb load:* 2,010 miles (3,235 km.). *Armament:* Two 0.303 in. Browning machine-guns in each of nose and dorsal turrets, and four more in tail turret; up to 14,000 lb. (6,350 kg.) of bombs internally.

67

Focke-Wulf Fw 200C-3/U1 *Condor* of I/KG.40 operating with *Fliegerführer Atlantik,* summer 1941. *Engines:* Four 1,200 h.p. Bramo 323R-2 Fafnir radials. *Span:* 107 ft. 9½ in. (30.855 m.). *Length:* 76 ft. 11½ in. (23.46 m.). *Height:* 20 ft. 8 in. (6.30 m.). *Maximum take-off weight:* 50,045 lb. (22,700 kg.). *Maximum speed:* 207 m.p.h. (333 km./hr.) at 15,750 ft. (4,800 m.). *Operational ceiling:* 19,030 ft. (5,800 m.). *Range (standard fuel):* 2,206 miles (3,550 km.). *Armament:* One 20 mm. MG 151/20 cannon in the front of the ventral gondola, one 15 mm. MG 151 machine-gun in forward dorsal turret, and three 7.9 mm. MG 15 guns (one in the rear of the ventral gondola and one in each beam position); up to 4,630 lb. (2,100 kg.) of bombs internally and externally.

FORTRESS (U.S.A.)

68

Boeing Fortress I (B-17C) of No. 90 Squadron RAF Bomber Command, summer 1941. *Engines:* Four 1,200 h.p. Wright R-1820-666C Cyclone radials. *Span:* 103 ft. 9⅜ in. (31.63 m.). *Length:* 67 ft. 10½ in. (20.69 m.). *Height:* 15 ft. 4½ in. (4.68 m.). *Normal take-off weight:* 47,500 lb. (21,546 kg.). *Maximum speed:* 325 m.p.h. (523 km./hr.) at 25,000 ft. (7,620 m.). *Operational ceiling:* 36,700 ft. (11,186 m.). *Maximum range:* 3,500 miles (5,633 km.). *Armament:* Six 0.50 in. Browning machine-guns (two each in dorsal and ventral positions, one in each beam position) and one 0.30 in. gun in nose; up to 4,000 lb. (1,814 kg.) of bombs internally.

84

FORTRESS (U.S.A.)

69

Douglas-built Boeing B-17F-60-DL of the 390th Bombing Group, US Eighth Air Force, UK 1943–45. *Engines:* Four 1,200 h.p. Wright R-1820-97 Cyclone radials. *Span:* 103 ft. 9$\frac{3}{8}$ in. (31.63 m.). *Length:* 74 ft. 8$\frac{7}{8}$ in. (22.78 m.). *Height:* 19 ft. 2$\frac{1}{2}$ in. (5.85 m.). *Normal take-off weight:* 55,000 lb. (24,948 kg.). *Maximum speed:* 299 m.p.h. (481 km./hr.) at 25,000 ft. (7,620 m.). *Operational ceiling:* 37,500 ft. (11,431 m.). *Range with 6,000 lb. (2,722 kg.) bomb load:* 1,300 miles (2,092 km.). *Armament:* Eight or nine 0.50 in. Browning machine-guns (two in forward dorsal turret, one in rear dorsal position (optional), two in ventral turret, two in tail turret and one in each beam position), and one 0.30 in. gun in nose; maximum permitted short-range load of 12,800 lb. (5,806 kg.) of bombs internally and 8,000 lb. (3,629 kg.) externally.

85

SUPERFORTRESS (U.S.A.)

70

Boeing B-29 Superfortress of the 795th Bomber Squadron, 468th Bomber Group, US 20th Air Force, CBI theatre early autumn 1944. *Engines:* Four 2,200 h.p. Wright R-3350-23 Cyclone radials. *Span:* 141 ft. 3 in. (43.05 m.). *Length:* 99 ft. 0 in. (30.18 m.). *Height:* 27 ft. 9 in. (8.46 m.). *Maximum take-off weight:* 135,000 lb. (61,235 kg.). *Maximum speed:* 357 m.p.h. (575 km./hr.) at 30,000 ft. (9,144 m.). *Operational ceiling:* 33,600 ft. (10,241 m.). *Range with 10,000 lb. (4,536 kg.) bomb load:* 3,250 miles (5,230 km.). *Armament:* One 20 mm. M2 cannon and two 0.50 in. machine-guns in tail turret; eight other 0.50 in. guns, two each in fore and aft dorsal and ventral turrets; up to 20,000 lb. (9,072 kg.) of bombs internally. **86**

LANCASTER (U.K.)

71

Avro Lancaster B I of No. 1661 Conversion Unit RAF, February 1944. *Engines:* Four 1,280 h.p. Rolls-Royce Merlin XX or 22 Vee type. *Span:* 102 ft. 0 in. (31.09 m.). *Length:* 69 ft. 4 in. (21.13 m.). *Height:* 19 ft. 7 in. (5.97 m.). *Maximum take-off weight:* 68,000 lb. (30,844 kg.). *Maximum speed:* 287 m.p.h. (462 km./hr.) at 11,500 ft. (3,505 m.). *Operational ceiling:* 24,500 ft. (7,467 m.). *Range with 12,000 lb. (5,443 kg.) bomb load:* 1,730 miles (2,784 km.). *Armament:* Eight 0.303 in. Browning machine-guns (two each in nose and dorsal turrets, four in tail turret); up to 18,000 lb. (8,165 kg.) of bombs internally.

72

Handley Page Halifax second prototype (representative of Mk I configuration), *ca.* September 1940. *Data apply to production Mk I Series I. Engines:* Four 1,075 h.p. Rolls-Royce Merlin X Vee type. *Span:* 98 ft. 10 in. (30.12 m.). *Length:* 70 ft. 1 in. (21.36 m.). *Height:* 20 ft. 9 in. (6.32 m.). *Maximum take-off weight:* 55,000 lb. (24,948 kg.). *Maximum speed:* 265 m.p.h. (426 km./hr.) at 17,500 ft. (5,334 m.). *Operational ceiling:* 22,800 ft. (6,949 m.). *Range with 5,800 lb. (2,631 kg.) bomb load:* 1,860 miles (2,993 km.). *Armament:* Two 0.303 in. Browning machine-guns in nose turret, four others in tail turret and (on some aircraft) two in beam positions; up to 13,000 lb. (5,897 kg.) of bombs internally.

73

Handley Page Halifax B III of No. 77 Squadron RAF Bomber Command, 1944. *Engines:* Four 1,615 h.p. Bristol Hercules XVI radials. *Span:* 104 ft. 2 in. (31.75 m.). *Length:* 71 ft. 7 in. (21.82 m.). *Height:* 20 ft. 9 in. (6.32 m.). *Normal take-off weight:* 54,400 lb. (24,675 kg.). *Maximum speed:* 282 m.p.h. (454 km./hr.) at 13,500 ft. (4,115 m.). *Operational ceiling:* 24,000 ft. (7,315 m.). *Range with maximum bomb load:* 1,030 miles (1,658 km.). *Armament:* Eight 0.303 in. Browning machine-guns (four each in dorsal and tail turrets) and one 0.303 in. Vickers K gun in nose; up to 13,000 lb. (5,897 kg.) of bombs internally.

LIBERATOR (U.S.A.)

74

Consolidated Liberator GR III (B-24D) of RAF Coastal Command, late 1943.
Engines: Four 1,200 h.p. Pratt & Whitney R-1830-43 Twin Wasp radials.
Span: 110 ft. 0 in. (33.53 m.). *Length:* 66 ft. 4 in. (20.22 m.). *Height:* 17 ft. 11 in.
(5.46 m.). *Maximum take-off weight:* 64,000 lb. (29,030 kg.). *Maximum speed:*
303 m.p.h. (488 km./hr.) at 25,000 ft. (7,620 m.). *Operational ceiling:* 32,000 ft.
(9,754 m.). *Maximum range:* 4,600 miles (7,403 km.). *Armament:* Two 0.50 in.
Browning machine-guns in dorsal turret, and seven 0.303 in. Browning guns
(one in nose, four in tail turret and one in each beam position); up to 8,000 lb.
(3,629 kg.) of bombs internally.

75

Convair B-24J-95-CO of the 448th Bombardment Group, US Eighth Air Force, UK *ca.* spring 1944. *Engines:* Four 1,200 h.p. Pratt & Whitney R-1830-65 Twin Wasp radials. *Span:* 110 ft. 0 in. (33.53 m.). *Length:* 67 ft. 2 in. (20.47 m.). *Height:* 17 ft. 7½ in. (5.37 m.). *Normal take-off weight:* 56,000 lb. (25,401 kg.). *Maximum speed:* 290 m.p.h. (467 km./hr.) at 25,000 ft. (7,620 m.). *Operational ceiling:* 28,000 ft. (8,534 m.). *Range at maximum overload weight of 64,500 lb. (29,257 kg.), including 5,000 lb. (2,268 kg.) bomb load:* 2,100 miles (3,380 km.). *Armament:* Ten 0.50 in. Browning machine-guns (two each in nose, tail, dorsal and ventral turrets and one in each beam position); normally up to 5,000 lb. (2,268 kg.) of bombs internally.

SUNDERLAND (U.K.)

76

Short Sunderland I of No. 210 (GR) Squadron RAF Coastal Command, 1940.
Engines: Four 1,010 h.p. Bristol Pegasus XXII radials. *Span:* 112 ft. 8 in.
(34.34 m.). *Length:* 85 ft. 8 in. (26.11 m.). *Height:* 32 ft. 10½ in. (10.02 m.).
Normal take-off weight: 44,600 lb. (20,230 kg.). *Maximum speed:* 210 m.p.h.
(338 km./hr.) at 6,500 ft. (1,981 m.). *Range with maximum load:* 1,780 miles
(2,865 km.). *Armament:* Four 0.303 in. Browning machine-guns in tail turret,
one 0.303 in. Vickers K or Lewis gun in nose turret, and two Vickers K guns
amidships; up to 2,000 lb. (907 kg.) of bombs internally.

KAWANISHI H8K (Japan)

77

Kawanishi H8K2 Model 12 of the JNAF Combined Maritime Escort Force, *ca.* 1944-45. *Engines:* Four 1,850 h.p. Mitsubishi Kasei 22 radials. *Span:* 124 ft. 8 in. (38.00 m.). *Length:* 92 ft. 3½ in. (28.13 m.). *Height:* 30 ft. 0¼ in. (9.15 m.). *Maximum take-off weight:* 71,650 lb. (32,500 kg.). *Maximum speed:* 290 m.p.h. (467 km./hr.) at 16,400 ft. (5,000 m.). *Operational ceiling:* 28,770 ft. (8,770 m.). *Maximum range:* 4,474 miles (7,200 km.). *Armament:* Two 20 mm. cannon in each of nose and tail turrets, one 20 mm. cannon in dorsal turret, and four 7.7 mm. machine-guns in beam blisters and on flight deck; up to eight 551 lb. (250 kg.) bombs or two 1,764 lb. (800 kg.) torpedos.

93

KAWANISHI H6K (Japan)

78

Kawanishi H6K4-L transport of No. 801 Air Corps JAAF, 1942. *Engines:* Four 1,070 h.p. Mitsubishi Kinsei 46 radials. *Span:* 131 ft. 2¾ in. (40.00 m.). *Length:* 84 ft. 1 in. (25.63 m.). *Height:* 20 ft. 6⅞ in. (6.27 m.). *Normal take-off weight:* 37,479 lb. (17,000 kg.). *Maximum speed:* 211 m.p.h. (340 km./hr.) at 13,120 ft. (4,000 m.). *Operational ceiling:* 31,530 ft. (9,610 m.). *Maximum range:* 2,535 miles (6,080 km.). *Armament* (*H6K4 patrol version only*): One 20 mm. cannon in tail turret, four 7.7 mm. machine-guns (one each in bow, dorsal and two beam positions); up to 3,527 lb. (1,600 kg.) of bombs internally or two 1,764 lb. (800 kg.) torpedos externally.

79

Messerschmitt Me 323D-1 (unit unknown), Eastern Front 1942–43. *Engines:* Six 990 h.p. Gnome-Rhône 14N 48/49 radials. *Data apply to Me 323D-6. Span:* 181 ft. 1¼ in. (55.20 m.). *Length:* 93 ft. 4½ in. (28.46 m.). *Height:* approximately 27 ft. 6 in. (8.38 m.). *Normal take-off weight:* 95,901 lb. (43,500 kg.). *Maximum speed:* 137 m.p.h. (220 km./hr.) at sea level. *Maximum payload:* 24,251 lb. (11,000 kg.). *Typical range:* 696 miles (1,120 km.). *Armament:* Five 13 mm. MG 131 machine-guns firing through apertures in nose-loading doors and from dorsal positions.

OHKA (Japan)

80

Yokosuka MXY-7 *Ohka* Model 11 piloted bomb, exhibited in the Indian Air Force Museum, New Delhi. *Engine:* One 1,764 lb. (800 kg.) st Type 4 Model 20 solid-propellant rocket motor. *Span:* 16 ft. 4$\frac{7}{8}$ in. (5.00 m.). *Length:* 19 ft. 10$\frac{7}{8}$ in. (6.07 m.). *Height:* approximately 3 ft. 11$\frac{1}{4}$ in. (1.20 m.). *Maximum weight:* 4,718 lb. (2,140 kg.). *Maximum level speed:* 534 m.p.h. (860 km./hr.). *Maximum diving speed:* 621 m.p.h. (1,000 km./hr.). *Range:* 55 miles (88 km.).

1 Supermarine Walrus

Originally in the Fleet reconnaissance role, and later as an air/sea rescue aeroplane, the Walrus amphibious flying boat was one of the best known sights in the wartime skies, especially those over British home waters. The Walrus could trace its lineage back to the Seagull amphibians of the 1920s, and when the prototype (K 4797) first appeared it was known as the Seagull V. It first flew on 21 June 1933, powered by a 635 hp Bristol Pegasus IIM.2 radial engine driving a pusher propeller. Twenty-four Seagull V's were ordered by the Australian Government, and a further twelve, to Specification 2/35, by the Fleet Air Arm, to whom it was known as the Walrus. In the following year Specification 36/37 was issued to cover another two hundred and four Walrus I's, and additional contracts followed later. Three from FAA orders were diverted to the Irish Army Air Corps in 1939. The metal-hulled Walrus I was delivered to FAA units from July 1936, initial allocations being made to battleships, cruisers and other warships equipped with catapults. These units were combined in January 1940 as No 700 Squadron, whose total aircraft strength included forty-two Walruses. Other Fleet-spotter squadrons to employ the Walrus included Nos 711, 712 and 714. From 1941 onward the Walrus was also employed increasingly by the Royal Air Force as an air/sea rescue amphibian, a task which it performed with distinction until the end of the war.

Seven RAF squadrons in Britain and four in the Middle East operated the Walrus in this role. From the two hundred and eighty-eighth machine onward production was undertaken by Saunders-Roe at Cowes with the designation Walrus II. The Saro-built aircraft had wooden hulls and Pegasus VI engines, and most of the ASR squadrons were equipped with this version. Despite its archaic appearance, the Walrus was a more rugged aeroplane than it seemed, and operated with utter reliability in sharply contrasted climates. Some operating in the Argentine were retired as recently as 1966.

2 Fairey Albacore

Two prototypes of the Albacore were built, to the requirements of Specification S.41/36 for a three-seat torpedo/spotter/reconnaissance aircraft for the FAA. The first of these (L 7074) flew on 12 December 1938, and production began in 1939 of the initial order for ninety-eight, placed in May 1937. When production ended in 1943 this total had increased to eight hundred and one. Early production Albacores, like the prototypes, were powered by Bristol Taurus II engines, but the 1,130 hp Taurus XII was installed in later batches; otherwise the 'Applecore' underwent comparatively little modification during its wartime career. This began with the formation of No 826 Squadron of the FAA specially to operate the Albacore, and the first dozen were officially accepted in mid-March 1940. The first operational sorties were made some ten weeks later, and in 1941 Albacores began to equip carrier-based FAA squadrons as well as those at shore stations. They subsequently gave extensive service in home waters and in the Mediterranean and Middle East theatres of war, until the arrival of Barracuda monoplane torpedo-bombers during 1943. At the peak of their career they equipped fifteen FAA squadrons, and figured in such major campaigns as the Battles of Cape Matapan and El Alamein, and the Allied landings in Sicily and at Salerno. When the last FAA squadron to fly Albacores (No 841) disbanded late in 1943 its aircraft were taken over by the Royal Canadian Air Force, in whose service they helped to keep the sea lanes open during the Allied invasion of Normandy in June 1944. Thus the Albacore, originally brought into being to replace the Fairey Swordfish, served alongside its sister aeroplane throughout its career and was actually retired from British service before the Swordfish.

3   Fairey Swordfish

Fortunately for the wartime Royal Navy, the loss of the Fairey T.S.R.I prototype in an accident in September 1933 was not sufficient to deter the Fairey Aviation Co from following it with a second, slightly larger development, the T.S.R.II. Designed, as its initials indicated, for the torpedo/spotter/reconnaissance role, the T.S.R.II (K 4190) was the true prototype of the later Swordfish and made its first flight on 17 April 1934. Delivery of production Swordfish to the FAA began in July 1936, the first recipient being No 825 Squadron. These were built to Specification S.38/34 and had the Pegasus IIIM.3 as power-plant. As an alternative to the 1,610 lb (730 kg) torpedo which it was designed to carry beneath the fuselage, the Swordfish I could carry a 1,500 lb (680 kg) mine in the same position or a similar total weight of bombs distributed under the fuselage and lower wings. Thirteen FAA squadrons were equipped with Swordfish at the outbreak of World War 2, a figure which was later almost doubled. At first they were employed largely on convoy or fleet escort duties, but in April 1940 the first major torpedo attack was made by Swordfish from HMS *Furious* during the Norwegian campaign, and their duties were soon extended to include mine-laying. Their most notable achievement was the destruction of three battleships, two destroyers, a cruiser and other warships of the Italian Fleet at Taranto on 10-11 November 1940, for the loss of only two Swordfish. The next variant was the Mk II, which appeared in 1943 and was built with metal-covered lower wings, enabling it to carry rocket projectiles. Later Mk II's were fitted with Pegasus XXX engines of 820 hp, and these also powered the Mk III, identifiable by its ASV radar housing beneath the front fuselage. Swordfish from all three Marks underwent conversion to Mk IV for service with the Royal Canadian Air Force; these were provided with enclosed cockpits. A substantial number of Mk I's were converted as twin-float seaplanes for service aboard catapult-equipped warships. The Swordfish was in action until less than four hours before the German surrender was signed, but after the war in Europe ended it was swiftly retired, the last FAA squadron disbanding on 21 May 1945. Total Swordfish production (including the prototype T.S.R.II) amounted to six hundred and ninety-two by Fairey and one thousand six hundred and ninety-nine by Blackburn. The Swordfish was universally known as the 'Stringbag' to all associated with it. Its lengthy and successful career, outlasting that of the Albacore which was meant to replace it, was a tribute to its excellent flying qualities, robust construction and uncomplaining adaptability.

4 Noorduyn Norseman

The first example of this Canadian 'bush' transport was completed in January 1935, and was then operated by Dominion Skyways, which later became a part of Canadian Pacific Air Lines. During the next five years Noorduyn sold only seventeen more of these aircraft, to commercial operators and to the Royal Canadian Mounted Police. Following the outbreak of World War 2, however, demand for military versions of this 9-seat utility transport increased spectacularly, both the RCAF and the USAAF placing orders. The former ordered thirty-eight Norseman Mk IV for radio and navigational training under the Empire Air Training Scheme. The USAAF, after evaluating seven

YC-64 Norsemen delivered in mid-1942, placed orders early in the following year for seven hundred and forty-six C-64A (later UC-64A) production aircraft; under Lend-Lease, thirty-four of these went to the RCAF as the Norseman VI, and forty-three others to various other Allied air forces; three others were diverted to the U.S. Navy with the designation JA-1. Plans for Aeronca also to build the C-64A were cancelled, but six C-64B floatplanes were ordered for the Engineering Corps, these all being delivered in 1943. Interchangeable wheel, ski or twin-float landing gear was available for all Norseman aircraft; the type was used by the U.S. forces mainly as a passenger or freight transport, but other duties included those of communications or casualty evacuation. Production of the Norseman by Noorduyn continued until 1946, when it was taken over by the Canadian Car and Foundry Company. The last of nine hundred and eighteen Norsemen was completed in January 1960. The post-war commercial version, the Norseman V (described in the *Private Aircraft* volume in this series), continues to be used in substantial numbers, alongside many demilitarised C-64A's.

5 Westland Lysander

Evolved to Specification A.39/34 for a 2-seat Army co-operation aeroplane, the Lysander was destined to play a far from passive role in the forthcoming war, and drew attention to its capabilities as early as

November 1939, when a Lysander shot down an He 111 bomber over France. The first of two Lysander prototypes (K 6127) flew on 15 June 1936, and in the following September one hundred and forty-four were ordered for the RAF under Specification 36/36. Deliveries, to No 16 Squadron, began in June 1938, and on 3 September 1939 the RAF had on charge sixty-eight Lysander Mk I and one hundred and ninety-five Mk II. Ultimately, one hundred and sixty-nine Mk I and four hundred and forty-two Mk II were completed. These differed principally in powerplant, the Mk I having an 890 hp Bristol Mercury XII and the Mk II a 905 hp Perseus XII. During wartime production of the Mks III (two hundred and sixty-seven) and IIIA (four hundred and forty-seven) many of these were built, and many earlier Lysanders converted, for service as target tugs. But the Lysander was to serve with distinction in roles of more direct value than these, notably those of air/sea rescue and agent-dropping. Here the low flying speeds and remarkable STOL characteristics of the Lysander provided a unique performance, especially for landing in and taking off from small fields or roads in Occupied Europe while fulfilling its 'cloak and dagger' role. Up to six bombs could be carried attached to the wheel fairings. All except the Mk IIIA carried only a single 0·303 in Lewis or Browning gun in the rear cockpit, but experimental versions with two 20-mm cannon or a four-gun Boulton Paul

turret were evolved in 1939. Other experimental Lysanders included the Steiger-wing P 9105, a converted Mk II, and the short-fuselage, tandem-wing project produced in 1941 by modifying the original prototype. Lysander production at Yeovil ended in January 1942, but an additional seventy-five Mk II and two hundred and fifty Mk III were built in Canada by the National Steel Car Corporation. Lysanders were supplied to Egypt (twenty), Eire (six), Finland (nine) and Turkey (thirty-six), and also served with the Free French and various Commonwealth air forces.

6 **Fieseler Fi 156 Storch (Stork)** Germany's counterpart to the Westland Lysander, the Fieseler Storch was also of pre-war design, three of the five prototypes being flown during 1936. A small pre-series batch of Fi 156A-0's was followed by the initial production model, the A-1, in 1938. No examples were completed of the Fi 156B, a projected civil version, and production continued with the Fi 156C series. The Fi 156C-0, which appeared early in 1939, introduced a defensive MG 15 machine-gun, mounted in a raised section at the rear of the 3-seat cabin, and was followed by C-1 staff transport and C-2 observation versions. All models thus far had been powered by Argus As 10C engines, but most of the multi-purpose C-3's built were fitted with the As 10P version of this engine. Detail improvements introduced during the production life of the C-3 were incorporated in

its successor, the C-5, which was able to carry such optional items as three 110-lb (50-kg) bombs, a 298-lb (135-kg) mine, a pod-mounted reconnaissance camera or an auxiliary drop-tank with which its range was increased to 628 miles (1,010 km). Final models were the Fi 156D-0 (As 10C) and Fi 156D-1 (As 10P), with increased cabin space and enlarged doors to permit the loading of a stretcher. From 1942 until the end of the war the C-5 and D-1 were the principal models in production. The Fi 156E-0 was a successful but experi-mental-only version with caterpillar-track landing gear for operation on rough or soft terrain. The Storch's remarkable STOL qualities enabled it to take off and land in extremely short distances, due to the full-span Handley Page wing leading-edge slats, and the slotted flaps and ailerons extending over the entire trailing edge. The wings could be folded back alongside the fuselage. Wartime production of the Storch, which amounted to two thousand five hundred and forty-nine aircraft, was transferred during 1944 to the Mraz factory in Czechoslovakia (which built sixty-four) and to the Morane-Saulnier works at Puteaux. The Storch served with the *Luftwaffe*, the *Regia Aeronautica* and in small numbers with the air forces of Bulgaria, Croatia, Finland, Hungary, Rumania, Slovakia and Switzerland. Both companies continued to build the type after the war, the Mraz version being known as the K-65 Cap (Stork) and the French version as the Criquet (Locust). The Fi 256 was a wartime Puteaux-built prototype for an enlarged 5-seat development.

7 Beriev MBR-2

In many ways the MBR-2 was to the Soviet Navy what the Super-marine Walrus was to the RAF and Fleet Air Arm, both types enjoying long production lives and service careers. The MBR-2 was designed by Georgi M. Beriev and flown in 1931, the functional letters in its designation indicating *Morskoi Blizhnii Razvedchik*, or Naval Short Range Reconnaissance. The proto-type was powered by an imported BMW VI.Z engine of 500 hp, and it was a licence-built development of this, the 680 hp M-17B, which powered the initial production version of the flying boat in 1934. This version carried a crew of four or five, with the two pilots seated side by side in an open cockpit; had open gun positions in the bow and midway along the top of the fuselage, each with a PV-1 machine-gun on a movable mounting; and was characterised by a square-topped fin and rudder. The flying boat, which became a standard Soviet Naval Aviation type during 1935, could also be fitted with a fixed wheel or ski landing gear, to enable it to operate from land or ice-covered waters. In 1934 an 8-passenger commercial version, designated MP-1, was put into service on internal routes by Aeroflot, and an MP-1T freighter counterpart ap-peared two years later. In 1935, however, an extensive redesign had been carried out by Beriev, based upon the installation of the more powerful Mikulin AM-34N engine. Other major changes included the provision of a manually operated dorsal turret, an enclosed crew cabin and larger, redesigned vertical tail surfaces. This version, sometimes referred to as the MBR-2bis, remained in production until 1941, and saw extensive service throughout World War 2. Many were still in service for fishery patrol and similar duties ten years later, and a few may still be flying today. The AM-34N-powered civil version was designated MP-1bis and entered Aeroflot service in 1937, after the prototype had been used to establish several distance and load-to-altitude records for women pilots.

8 Aichi D3A

Aichi was one of three companies to compete, in 1936, for the Imperial Japanese Navy's 11-Shi requirement for a new carrier-borne dive bomber, and its design showed strongly the influence of current German products by Heinkel, with whom the Japanese Navy had a clandestine agreement. Aichi's design was awarded a development contract, and entered production in 1937 as the D3A1 Model 11, or Type 99 carrier-based dive bomber. The Model 11 remained in production until August 1942; it was a standard JNAF type at the time of the attack on Pearl Harbor (in which it took part), and in April 1942 the British carrier *Hermes* and the cruisers *Cornwall* and *Dorsetshire* were sunk in the Indian Ocean by D3A1's. A single 250 kg bomb could be carried on a ventral cradle which was swung forward and downward to clear the propeller during delivery, and a 60 kg bomb could be attached to each outer wing section. After delivering its bombs the D3A1 was sufficiently well armed and manoeuvrable to put up a creditable fight against the Allied fighters then in service. Four hundred and seventy-eight D3A1's were built, production then continuing with the D3A2 Model 22 until January 1944, when eight hundred and sixteen D3A2's had been completed. The D3A2 introduced cockpit and minor airframe improvements, but differed chiefly in having a 1,300 hp Kinsei 54 engine which raised the maximum speed to 266 mph (428 kmh) at 18,540 ft (5,650 m). Normal and maximum take-off weights of this model were 8,378 lb (3,800 kg) and 9,088 lb (4,122 kg) respectively, and the maximum range 1,572 miles (2,530 km). Both the D3A1 and the D3A2 (which were code named 'Val' by the Allies) figured prominently in the major Pacific battles, including those of Santa Cruz, Midway and the Solomon Islands; but increasing losses, both of aircraft and of experienced pilots, progressively reduced their contribution to the Japanese war effort, and during the second half of the Pacific War they were encountered much less often. Some were converted as single-seat suicide attack aircraft, and a number of D3A2's were adapted for the training role with the designation D3A2-K.

9 Arado Ar 196

Possessing a general appearance similar to many of the Arado biplanes of the immediate pre-war years, the Arado Ar 196 monoplane entered service in the month preceding the outbreak of World War 2. Its design had been started some years earlier, as a replacement for the obsolescent Heinkel He 60 catapult biplanes then carried by German capital ships, and during 1938 two twin-float prototypes (the Ar 196V1 and V2), and two others (the V3 and V4) with one centrally mounted main float, were flown. Towards the end of 1938 production was started at Warnemünde of the Ar 196A-1. Apart from replacement of the 880 hp BMW 132Dc radial (which had powered all four prototypes) by the more powerful BMW 132K, the Ar 196A-1 basically resembled the V2 prototype, the smaller fin and horn-balanced rudder of the V1 having been discarded in favour of a more typical Arado empennage. The Ar 196A-1 was armed with single forward- and rearward-firing 7·9 mm MG 17 machine-guns, one fixed in the front fuselage and the other on a flexible mount in the aft cockpit. The Ar 196A-1's, twenty-six of which were completed during 1939, were deployed chiefly aboard such major warships as the *Bismarck, Gneisenau, Graf Spee, Lützow, Scharnhorst* and *Scheer,* and at shore-based training establishments. In 1940 the initial version began to be joined by the principal production version, the Arado Ar 196A-3. This had improved internal equipment, but was notable chiefly for its augmented armament. When they first entered service the Ar 196A-3's operated from newly acquired bases in France, and were frequently used against Allied anti-submarine patrols in the Biscay area until countered by the appearance of the Beaufighter. Thereafter they themselves were used for anti-submarine patrols, and for convoy escort and reconnaissance, from seaplane shore bases in the Mediterranean theatre (notably Crete). The only other known operational version was the Ar 196A-5, which differed from the A-3 simply in internal equipment. Sixty-nine examples of this model were completed by Fokker in the Netherlands during 1943-44. Production by Arado, which ceased in 1943, amounted to four hundred and one aircraft, the great majority of which were the A-3 model. A further twenty-three A-3's were completed in 1942-43 by the Sud-Ouest factory at St Nazaire in Vichy France. *Luftwaffe* units employing the Ar 196 included *Seeaufklärungsgruppen* 125 and 126 and *Bordfliegergruppe* 196. Small numbers of Ar 196A-3's were also in service in the Adriatic during the war, with the air forces of Rumania and Bulgaria. The Ar 196V3, with its central main float and outer stabilising floats, was intended to serve as prototype for a proposed Ar 196B production model following this configuration, but which proved to be unnecessary. The V4 was used for armament trials.

10 Nakajima B5N

The B5N was designed by Nakajima to a 10-Shi (1935) requirement by the JNAF for a carrier-based attack bomber. It exhibited several advanced features for its time, and its design was influenced in no small part by the Northrop 5A, an example of which had arrived in Japan in 1935. The prototype B5N1 flew for the first time in January 1937, and was a clean-looking 2/3-seat monoplane with mechanically folding wings, Fowler-type landing flaps and a fully retractable main undercarriage. Its 770 hp Hikari 3 radial engine was installed beneath a neat NACA cowling, and on test the prototype aircraft exceeded the performance specification in many respects. The B5N1 Model 11 entered production late in 1937, and saw combat service in the Sino-Japanese conflict that preceded Japan's entry into World War 2. The B5N1 was armed with a single defensive machine-gun at the rear. Production of the B5N1 was simplified by adopting manual instead of mechanical wing-folding, and by substituting slotted flaps for the Fowler type. Late production aircraft (designated Model 12) were fitted with 985 hp Sakae 11 engines. A prototype appeared in December 1939 of the B5N2 Model 23, a torpedo bomber version powered by a 1,115 hp Sakae 21 engine. This was armed with two forward-firing guns and one or two guns in the rear cockpit; and it could carry an 18 in torpedo or bombs under the fuselage. The B5N2 entered JNAF service in 1940, and both variants were con-cerned in the attack on Pearl Harbor in December 1941. Subsequently they were responsible for the destruction of several other major U.S. carriers during the early part of the war. The B5N, known by the Allied code name 'Kate', was encountered operationally as late as June 1944, when a number were engaged in the Marianas Islands campaign. For a year or more, however, the B5N had been obsolescent, and indeed several B5N1's were withdrawn from operations and converted to B5N1-K trainers soon after the B5N2 began to enter service. More than one thousand two hundred 'Kates' were completed, some of them by Aichi, before the B5N began to be superseded by its newer and faster stablemate, the B6N Tenzan. A number of B5N's were, however, employed as suicide aircraft in the final stages of the war.

11 Douglas SBD Dauntless

Evolution of the Dauntless began in 1934, when a Northrop team under Ed Heinemann based a new Navy dive-bomber design on the company's Army A-17A. Designated XBT-1, it flew in July 1935, and in February 1936 fifty-four BT-1's with 825 hp R-1535-94 engines were ordered. The last of these was completed as the XBT-2, with a 1,000 hp R-1820-32 engine. With further modifications, notably to the landing gear and vertical tail contours, this was redesignated XSBD-1 when Northrop was absorbed by Douglas on 31 August 1937. At about this time the perforated dive flaps, a distinctive Dauntless feature, were introduced. Delivery of fifty-seven SBD-1's to the Marine Corps began in mid-1940. Simultaneously, the U.S. Navy ordered eighty-seven SBD-2's with additional fuel, protective armour and autopilots. Both versions were armed with two 0·30 in machine-guns in the upper engine cowling and a single 0·30 in gun in the rear cockpit. Bombs up to 1,000 lb (454 kg) in size could be carried on an under-fuselage cradle; maximum bomb load was 1,200 lb (544 kg). Delivery of SBD-2's, from November 1940, was followed from March 1941 by one hundred and seventy-four SBD-3's, with R-1820-52 engines and 0·50 in front guns. The two models were standard U.S. Navy carrier-borne dive-bombers at the time of Pearl Harbor; subsequently, the Navy received a further four hundred and ten SBD-3's. In May 1942 SBD pilots from the USS *Lexington* and *Yorktown* were credited with forty of the ninety-one enemy aircraft lost during the Battle of the Coral Sea; a month later, at Midway, SBD's from the *Enterprise*, *Hornet* and *Yorktown* sank the Japanese carriers *Akagi*, *Kaga* and *Soryu* and put the *Hiryu* out of action. Their own attrition rate was the lowest of any U.S. carrier aircraft in the Pacific, due largely to an outstanding ability to absorb battle damage, and the Dauntless at this time did more than any other type to turn the tide of the war in the Pacific. Later, Dauntlesses continued the war from the decks of escort carriers, flying anti-submarine or close-support missions with depth charges or rocket projectiles. In October 1942 delivery began of seven hundred and eighty SBD-4's fitted with radar and radio-navigation equipment. They were followed by the major production model, the SBD-5, with increased engine power. To the two thousand nine hundred and sixty-five SBD-5's for the U.S. Navy were added sixty SBD-5A's, built to an Army contract but delivered instead to the Marine Corps. One SBD-5, with a 1,350 hp R-1820-66 engine, acted as a prototype for the four hundred and fifty SBD-6's which completed Dauntless production in July 1944. Overall production amounted to five thousand nine hundred and thirty-six, the balance consisting of one hundred and sixty-eight A-24's and six hundred and fifteen A-24B's for the USAAF, delivered from June 1941. These corresponded to the SBD-3 and -3A, SBD-4 and SBD-5 respectively, but had new tailwheels, internal equipment changes and no arrester gear. The Army machines were not flown with a great degree of combat success, and were used chiefly for training or communications. The Royal New Zealand Air Force received eighteen SBD-3's, twenty-seven SBD-4's and twenty-three SBD-5's. Thirty-two SBD-5's were supplied to the French Navy, and between forty and fifty A-24B's to the *Armée de l'Air*; but the latter, like their U.S. Army counterparts, were employed mainly on second-line duties. Nine SBD-5's were delivered to the British Fleet Air Arm, but were not used operationally.

12 Yokosuka D4Y Suisei (Comet)

When the prototype D4Y1 made its first flight in November 1940 it became the first Japanese Navy aircraft since 1932 to fly with an in-line engine. The Navy's 1937 specification, to which it was designed, had called for a 2-seat, carrier-based dive bomber with a range of 920-1,380 miles (1,480-2,220 km) and a speed as fast as the A6M2 Zero fighter. Yokosuka's design proposed an aeroplane with a comparatively small airframe, in which the minimal frontal area of an in-line engine was an important factor. The prototype was powered by an imported Daimler-Benz DB 600G of 960 hp; production D4Y1's by the 1,200 hp Aichi Atsuta 21. Apart from five hundred completed by the Hiro Naval Air Arsenal, Aichi also built all of the two thousand three hundred and nineteen D4Y's that were produced. The D4Y1 Model 11 entered production early in 1941, but when various structural weaknesses became apparent during service this was supplanted by the strengthened D4Y2 with the Atsuta 32 engine. Delivery of Atsuta engines, however, fell behind the airframe production date, and gave rise to the D4Y3 Model 33, in which a change was made to the 1,560 hp Mitsubishi Kinsei 62 radial engine. Some loss of performance with this engine was accepted as the price for virtual elimination, in the D4Y3, of undercarriage retraction difficulties and other problems encountered in earlier models. The Suisei first appeared operationally in a recon-naissance role, designated D4Y1-C, when aircraft from the carrier *Soryu* took part in the Battle of Midway Island. The D4Y2 was used initially as a dive bomber, but by the time of the Marianas campaign in September 1944 – its first major action – this also (as the D4Y2-C) had become used for reconnaissance. By the time the radial-engined D4Y3 appeared, Japanese carrier losses were such that the 'Judy' (as the D4Y was coded by the Allies) operated almost equally from shore bases. During the final year of the war there appeared the D4Y4 Model 43, a single-seat conversion of the D4Y3 adapted for suicide attacks with 1,764 lb (800 kg) of high explosive on board; and a number of Model 12's were converted to D4Y2-S emergency night fighters for home defence in 1945. These had one or two 20 mm cannon placed behind the rear cockpit to fire obliquely forward and upward.

13 Grumman TBF Avenger

The Avenger was a pre-war design, two XTBF-1 prototypes of which were ordered by the U.S. Navy in April 1940. The first of these made its maiden flight on 1 August 1941, by which time a substantial first order had been placed. The first production TBF-1's were delivered to Squadron VT-8 late in January 1942, and the Avenger made its combat debut early in the following June at the Battle of Midway. The aircraft had typical Grumman lines, the most noticeable feature being the very deep fuselage, which enabled the torpedo or bomb load to be totally enclosed. The TBF-1C had two wing-mounted 0·50 in machine-guns in addition to the nose, dorsal and ventral guns of the original TBF-1, and could carry auxiliary drop-tanks. Both models were 3-seaters and were powered by the 1,700 hp R-2600-8 engine. Up to December 1943 Grumman built two thousand two hundred and ninety-three TBF-1/-1C Avengers, including the two original prototypes, one XTBF-2 and one XTBF-3. Four hundred and two of them were supplied to the Royal Navy as Avenger Mk I's (=TBF-1B) and sixty-three to the RNZAF. The British aircraft were briefly known as Tarpons, but the U.S. name was later standardised. Meanwhile, in the U.S.A. production had also begun in September 1942 by the Eastern Aircraft Division of General Motors, which built two thousand eight hundred and eighty-two as the TBM-1 and -1C. Three hundred and thirty-four of these went to the Royal Navy as Avenger II's. The 'dash two' variant was not built by either company, but Eastern completed a prototype and four thousand six hundred and sixty-four TBM-3's with uprated Cyclone engines and their wings strengthened to carry rocket projectiles or a radar pod. Two hundred and twenty-two of these became the British Avenger III. Further strengthening of the airframe produced the XTBM-4, but production of this model was cancelled when the war ended. This did not, however, end the Avenger's long and productive career: those

of the U.S. Navy were not finally retired until 1954, and post-war variants served with some foreign naval air forces for several years after this. During the major part of World War 2 the Avenger was the standard U.S. Navy torpedo-bomber, operating alike from carriers or shore bases, mostly in the Pacific theatre.

14 **Sukhoi Su-2**
While a member of the Tupolev design collective, Pavel Sukhoi designed a low-wing, single-engined bomber designated ANT-51. Test flights of this aeroplane, which began in August 1937, were disappointing, but Sukhoi continued to develop the basic concept after establishing his own design bureau early in 1939. Three prototypes were completed and flown, with 950 hp M-87A, M-87B and M-88 engines respectively, and the third version was accepted for production in 1940 with the functional designation BB-1. The production BB-1 had a well-armoured cockpit and crew of two, and the internal weapons bay could, if necessary, contain the entire 1,323 lb (600 kg) bomb load. More usually, however, the internal load was restricted to 882 lb (400 kg), the remaining weapons (bombs or rocket projectiles) being distributed under the wings. Early in 1941 the uprated M-88B engine began to be installed, and with the revision of the Soviet designation system the BB-1 became known as the Su-2. During the early period of the Nazi attack on the U.S.S.R. the Su-2 was in fairly widespread use, but it was

no match for the *Luftwaffe's* superior fighters, and after about a hundred Su-2's had been completed (some with twin dorsal guns) an attempt was made to improve its performance to bridge the gap until the Ilyushin Il-2 became available in quantity. Protective crew armour was increased, but the major alteration was the introduction of the 1,400 hp Shvetsov M-82 engine, which became the standard powerplant until production ceased during the latter half of 1942. Despite the numbers produced, the installation of the M-82 engine proved a retrograde step, for, while it improved the Su-2's performance on paper, its higher installed weight upset the aircraft's handling characteristics. Combat losses continued to be high, and the Su-2 was withdrawn from operational units from 1942 onward. An Su-2 re-engined with a 2,100 hp M-90 radial was test-flown in 1941 with the designation Su-4. A much superior development was the ground-attack Su-6, but as a contemporary of the already-established Il-2, this did not go into large-scale production.

15 Curtiss SB2C Helldiver

The XSB2C-1 Helldiver prototype, following its first flight on 18 December 1940, was lost in a crash early in the following year – an inauspicious beginning to the career of perhaps the most successful dive bomber ever to enter U.S. Navy service. The initial Navy order, placed in November 1940, was later increased until nine hundred and seventy-eight SB2C-1's had been completed, the first of which was delivered in June 1942. They were succeeded by one thousand one hundred and twelve SB2C-3's, two thousand and forty-five SB2C-4's and nine hundred and seventy SB2C-5's. The SB2C-3 had the 1,900 hp R-2600-20 model of the Cyclone engine, while the SB2C-4 introduced search radar in an under-wing fairing and provision for an external warload of 1,000 lb (454 kg) of bombs or eight 5 in rocket projectiles. The SB2C-5 was essentially a longer-range variant of the -4. Nine hundred Helldivers purchased by the USAAF, and built by Curtiss and Douglas with the Army title A-25A Shrike, were mostly transferred to the Marine Corps as SB2C-1A's. Starting in the summer of 1943 the Canadian Car and Foundry Co built eight hundred and ninety-four SBW-1, -3, -4 and -5 Helldivers, including twenty-six supplied to the British Fleet Air Arm. Fairchild in Canada contributed three hundred SBF-1, -3 and -4 versions to bring the overall Helldiver production total to seven thousand two hundred aircraft. The British machines were not used on active service, but the American Helldivers, perpetuating the name given to Curtiss's earlier SBC biplane dive bomber, played a prominent part in the Pacific war, operating from the USS *Bunker Hill*, *Enterprise*, *Essex*, *Independence* and other carriers. Their first major action was the Rabaul campaign in November 1943, and they took part in virtually every major naval/air action during the rest of the war. One SB2C-1 was fitted experimentally with twin floats as the XSB2C-2, and an SB2C-5 with 2,100 hp R-2600-22 engine became the sole XSB2C-6, but neither version went into production.

16 Nakajima B6N Tenzan

Just as Nakajima's earlier B5N attack bomber had exhibited superiority over most of its Allied contemporaries, so did its successor, the B6N, despite the engine troubles encountered early in its career. Only the lack of a carrier fleet and sufficient experienced pilots by the JNAF prevented the B6N from being a more serious threat to Allied shipping during the later part of the war. The powerplant chosen for the B6N1, which flew in prototype form in March 1942, was the 1,870 hp Nakajima Mamori II. Despite the bulk of this powerful two-row radial engine, it was installed in a close-fitting cowling that did little to mar the outstandingly clean lines of the B6N design. However, the engine was prone to overheating and vibration, which eventually caused the B6N1 Model 11 to be withdrawn from production, though not from service. It was superseded by the B6N2 Model 12, powered by the more reliable Mitsubishi Kasei 25, which offered a lighter installed weight and more straightforward maintenance for only a slight reduction in output. The B6N was named Tenzan by the Japanese, after a Chinese mountain, and in the Allied code naming system was known as 'Jill'. The B6N1 carried dorsal and ventral machine-guns,

the latter gun being extended into the airstream after the torpedo had been releasedt, to discourage anti-aircraft fire from the ship just attacked. In the B6N2 an additional forward-firing gun was provided in one wing. To avoid fouling the bombs or torpedo, the oil cooler was offset to port on the lower portion of the engine cowling. First combat appearance of the Tenzan was in December 1943, when a group of B6N1's attacked a U.S. task force off the Marshall Islands, but most of the one thousand two hundred and sixty-eight Tenzans built at Nakajima's Handa and Koizumi factories were B6N2's. This version made its first operational appearance in the Marianas campaign in June 1944, and was encountered again in engagements in the Caroline and Solomon Islands groups and at Iwo Jima. Tenzans carrying ASV radar attacked Allied naval concentrations off Kyushu in March 1945, and from April to June 1945 the JNAF mounted a considerable torpedo and suicide attack campaign with Tenzans against Allied ships in the vicinity of Okinawa.

17 Fairey Barracuda

The ungainly form of the Barracuda, and its 'Christmas-tree' appearance when bedecked with torpedos, bombs, lifeboats, radar arrays and the like, were the direct outcome of the exacting Specification S.24/37 to which it was designed. It was the first British carrier-based monoplane torpedo bomber of all-metal construction, yet its high, strut-braced tailplane and large, Fairey-Youngman trailing-edge flaps might have suggested to the uninitiated a less sophisticated design than was actually the case. Abandonment of the intended Rolls-Royce Exe engine delayed the trials of the first prototype (P 1767), which eventually flew on 7 December 1940 with a 1,260 hp Merlin 30. Priority afforded to other types of aircraft then delayed production, the first Barracuda I not being flown until 18 May 1942. Thirty of this model were completed (including five by Westland), and they were followed by one thousand six hundred and eighty-eight Barracuda II's with the uprated Merlin 32, which permitted higher operating weights but slightly reduced the overall performance. The Barracuda I's were used chiefly for trials or conversion training, the first operational unit being No 827 Squadron, which received the Mk II in January 1943. First combat action was with No 810 Squadron during the Salerno landings eight months later. In service, the Barracuda was more often employed as a dive bomber than with a torpedo, and it was in this role that forty-two Barracudas, from four Squadrons aboard the carriers *Victorious* and *Furious*, carried out the attack on the *Tirpitz* in *Kaafioord* in northern Norway in April 1944, scoring fifteen direct hits on the German battleship with armour-piercing 500 lb and 1,000 lb bombs for the loss of only three Barracudas. Later that month Barracudas from *Illustrious* carried out the type's first combat action in the Pacific theatre. Final wartime

version was the Mk III, with a ventral ASV radome for anti-submarine patrols but otherwise generally similar to the Mk II. Fairey built six hundred and seventy-five Mk II's, Blackburn seven hundred, Boulton Paul three hundred and Westland thirteen. Four hundred and sixty Mk III's were built by Fairey, and three hundred and ninety-two by Boulton Paul. One Mk II was re-engined with a 1,850 hp Griffon VII as prototype for the unarmed Mk V (the Mk IV was not built), and this aircraft (P 9976) flew on 16 November 1944. Thirty production Mk V's, with tail surfaces and other features extensively redesigned, were built by Fairey, with 2,020 hp Griffon 37's, but were not completed until after the war and served mainly as trainers.

18 Fairey Battle

Often, when a particular aeroplane type is utilised as a flying test-bed for a variety of experimental engines, such employment is an indication that its general handling qualities are rather above the average. Such was the case with the Battle, several examples of which were employed in this fashion to air-test various engines of up to 2,000 hp. This was a considerable increase over the 1,030 hp of the Merlin I that powered the prototype (K 4303) when it made its first flight on 10 March 1936. The Battle was designed by Marcel Lobelle to Specification P.27/32 for a 2-seat day bomber to replace the Hawker Hart biplane, and an initial order for one hundred and fifty-five Battles, to Specification P.23/35, was placed before the prototype had flown. The first production Battle was completed in June 1937, and the bomber – now a 3-seater – was one of the types chosen for large-scale priority production as part of the RAF expansion programme. Under the 'shadow factory' scheme Austin Motors shared the production with Fairey, and on 3 September 1939 the RAF had well over a thousand Battle Mks I-III on charge. (Production Battles were powered successively by Merlin Mk I, II, III or V engines, and took their own Mark numbers from that of the engine. This famous engine series first entered production as the powerplant for the Battle.) Ultimately, Fairey built one thousand one hundred and fifty-six Battles, and Austin one thousand and twenty-nine; an additional eighteen were completed before the war by Avions Fairey in Belgium. First RAF deliveries were made to No 63 Squadron in May 1937, and on 2 September 1939 ten Battle squadrons flew to France as part of the Advanced Air Striking Force. Normal bomb load was stowed in four cells in the wings, but this could be increased to a maximum of 1,500 lb (680 kg) by carrying extra bombs on under-wing racks. Many brave actions were fought by Battle crews, but the bomber was already outdated by the time the war started and was no match for the *Luftwaffe* fighters ranged against it. Consequently, it was soon withdrawn to non-combatant duties, such as operational training and target towing. In the former role it flew also with the air forces of Australia, Canada and South Africa, and pre-war exports also included twenty-nine for the Turkish Air Force. The type was finally withdrawn from RAF service in 1949.

19 **Junkers Ju 87**
The United States and Germany, in particular, were enthusiastic proponents of the dive bomber during the later 1930s and the early part of World War 2. This particular species of warplane seemed to be typified in the Ju 87, whose ugly lines and wailing engine struck an especial note of terror in the skies above Poland, France and the Low Countries in 1939–40. Design of the Ju 87, by Dipl-Ing Pohlmann, started in 1933, and the first prototype flew early in 1935. This was powered by a Rolls-Royce Kestrel engine and had rectangular twin fins and rudders, but the Ju 87V2, flown in the following autumn, had a single tail and a 610 hp Junkers Jumo 210A engine, and was more representative of the production aircraft to follow. A pre-series batch of Ju 87A-0's was started in 1936, and in the spring of 1937 delivery began of the Ju-87A-1 initial production model, followed by the generally similar A-2. About two hundred A series were built before, in the autumn of 1938, there appeared the much-modified Ju 87B. Powered by the Jumo 211, this had an enlarged vertical tail, redesigned crew canopy and new-style cantilever fairings over the main legs of

the landing gear. Both the A and B models were sent for service with the Condor Legion in Spain in 1938, but by the outbreak of World War 2 the A series had been relegated to the training role, and the three hundred and thirty-six aircraft in front-line service were all Ju 87B-1's. The fighter superiority of the *Luftwaffe* ensured the Ju 87 a comparatively uninterrupted passage in 1939–40, but opposition during the Battle of Britain was much sterner, and losses of the Ju 87 were considerably heavier. Nevertheless, production of the B series continued into 1941, and substantial numbers were supplied to the *Regia Aeronautica*, and to the air forces of Bulgaria, Hungary and Rumania. In production alongside the B series was the long-range Ju 87R, which from 1940 was used for anti-shipping and other missions. Before the war small numbers were also completed of the Ju 87C, a version of the B with arrester hook, folding wings and other 'navalised' attributes. This was planned for service aboard the carrier *Graf Zeppelin*, but the ship was never completed, and the few Ju 87C-0's built served with a land-based unit. Others laid down as C-1's were completed as B-2's. After the setbacks in the Battle of Britain the Ju 87B continued to serve in the Mediterranean and North Africa. Its subsequent development and employment was mainly in the close-support role or as a trainer; these versions are described in the companion volume *Fighters, Attack and Training Aircraft 1939–45*.

20 **Nakajima C6N Saiun (Colourful Cloud)**
The Saiun was designed by Yasuo Fukuda to a 17-Shi (1942) requirement for a carrier-based reconnaissance aircraft. Originally, Fukuda contemplated the use of two 1,000 hp radial engines mounted in tandem, but a single, small-diameter Homare engine, which promised to develop around 2,000 hp, was chosen instead. To shorten the Saiun's development period, no less than twenty-three prototypes were ordered, and many of these were completed by the end of 1943. Several of the prototypes were assigned to active units as part of the test programme, and it was they that made the aircraft's operational debut. The Saiun, to which the Allies gave the code name 'Myrt', was first encountered in June 1944, when a number of these aircraft made a reconnaissance of the U.S. task force assembling for the attack on the Marianas Islands. Later the Saiun also reconnoitred the force being assembled to attack Saipan. Series production of the Saiun, as the C6N1 Model 11, began in 1944, the first deliveries to JNAF units being made in August. By the end of the war Nakajima's Handa and Koizumi factories had built four hundred and ninety-eight Saiuns, but their service career was delayed and interrupted by continual troubles with the problematical Homare engine, and they were not met in large numbers. The light armament of the reconnaissance version reflected the aircraft's ability to outpace and outclimb most of

the late-war Allied fighters, but those converted for other roles were more comprehensively equipped. The C6N1-S was a home defence night fighter, with a crew of two and twin 20 mm cannon fixed in the rear fuselage to fire obliquely forward and upward. The C6N1-B was a 3-seat torpedo bomber conversion. Two prototypes were also completed of an improved reconnaissance variant, the C6N2 Model 22, powered by the 2,000 hp Homare 24 engine. The final development, designated C6N3 Saiun-Kai, was to have been powered by a Hitachi 92 engine, but this had only reached the project stage when the war ended.

21 Heinkel He 115

It was to be expected that Ernst Heinkel, designer of several fine marine aircraft during World War 1, should produce one of the leading seaplanes of the 1939-45 conflict. The first He 115 prototype (D-AEHF) flew in 1936, being modified later for attempts on the prevailing world seaplane speed records, eight of which it captured on 20 March 1938. The definitive production aircraft was fore-shadowed by the third and fourth prototypes, with an extensively glazed nose and long 'greenhouse' canopy, and, in the latter case, no wire bracing for the twin floats. Ten pre-production He 115A-0's and thirty-four He 115A-1's were completed in 1937 and 1938 respectively, the latter having an MG 15 gun in the nose as well as the observer's dorsal gun. The A-2 was the export

equivalent of the *Luftwaffe's* A-1, and was sold to Norway (six) and Sweden (ten). The first large-scale domestic version, the He 115A-3, was soon followed by the He 115B series, comprising ten B-0's and fifty-two B-1/B-2's. These had increased fuel capacity and could carry one of Hitler's much-vaunted 'secret weapons', the magnetic mine, in addition to their internal bomb load. With these they caused considerable havoc to Allied shipping during the early years of the war. In 1940-41 there appeared the He 115C series, of which the C-0, C-1 and C-2 sub-types had an extra forward-firing 20 mm MG 151 cannon in a fairing under the nose. On some aircraft, a 7·9 mm MG 17 gun was installed in each wing root as well. The C series concluded with eighteen C-3 minelayers and thirty C-4 torpedo bombers, the latter having the dorsal MG 15 as its only defensive gun. One He 115A-1 was re-engined with 1,600 hp BMW 801C radials and equipped with five machine-guns and a cannon to become the He 115D; but although this was used operationally, no production of the D series was undertaken. In fact, all production was halted for a time, but was resumed in 1943-44 to build one hundred and forty-one examples of the E-0 and E-1 variants, bringing the overall total to about four hundred aircraft. These were similar to earlier models except for variations in armament. Two of the Norwegian A-2's, which escaped to Britain after the invasion of Norway in 1940, were later employed in RAF colours to transport Allied agents between Malta and North Africa.

22 Vickers Wellington

On 3 September 1939 the RAF had one hundred and seventy-nine Wellingtons on strength, rather less than the number of Hampdens or Whitleys, but these three types bore the brunt of Bomber Command's operations during the early part of the war until the arrival of the four-engined heavy bombers from 1941. The Wellington went on to outstrip both of its contemporaries, an ultimate total of eleven thousand four hundred and sixty-one being built before production ceased in October 1945. After being withdrawn from Bomber Command in 1943, Wellingtons began a second career with Coastal Command as maritime reconnaissance aircraft, at home and in the Middle and Far East; others were employed briefly as transports and (after the war) as aircrew trainers. The 'Wimpey' was designed to Specification B.9/32, the prototype (K 4049) flying on 15 June 1936. Considerable redesign of the fuselage and vertical tail was evident in the production aircraft, ordered to Specification 29/36. The first of these was flown on 23 December 1937, and the first Wellington squadron was No 9, which received its aircraft in October 1938. Those in service when war broke out were Pegasus-engined Mks I or IA, but the most numerous early model was the Mk IC, of which two thousand six hundred and eighty-five were built. Prototypes had also flown before the war

of the Merlin-engined Mk II and the Mk III with Bristol Hercules radials. Wellingtons of Nos 9 and 149 Squadrons, in company with Blenheims, carried out the RAF's first bombing attack of the war when they bombed German shipping at Brunsbüttel. From mid-December 1939 they were switched to night bombing only, joining in the first raid on Berlin late in August 1940. In the following month they made their Middle East debut, and appeared in the Far East from early 1942. By this time the Mk III (one thousand five hundred and nineteen built) was the principal service version, although two squadrons operated the Twin Wasp-engined Mk IV. The first general reconnaissance version for Coastal Command, the Mk VIII, appeared in the spring of 1942. Three hundred and ninety-four, with similar engines to the Mk IC, were built. They were followed by substantial batches of the Mks XI, XII, XIII and XIV, with differing versions of the Hercules and variations in operational equipment. Overseas, the Wellington maintained its combat role, the Mk X in particular (three thousand eight hundred and four built) serving with the Middle East Air Forces as well as with Bomber Command. Wellingtons of No 40 Squadron made a bombing attack on Treviso, Italy, as late as March 1945. Other Wellingtons were converted as torpedo bombers, minelayers and transports, and a special variant designated D.W.1 was fitted with a large electro-magnetic 'degaussing' ring to trigger off enemy mines. The light but extremely strong geodetic method of the Wellington's construction not only enabled it to carry a creditable bomb load but was capable of withstanding a considerable amount of battle damage without failure.

23 Heinkel He 111

In one form or another, the He 111's service career extended over more than thirty years, an outstanding tribute to the design, evolved by the Günter brothers early in 1934. Of the original four prototypes, the first was flown on 24 February 1935, and the second and fourth were completed ostensibly as civilian transports. Bomber production was heralded in the summer of 1935 by the He 111V4 and a pre-series batch of He 111A-0's, but their BMW engines provided insufficient power, and the first major type was the He 111B, with DB 600-series engines. This was one of the most successful types to serve with the Condor Legion in Spain, where it was fast enough to fly unescorted. To preserve supplies of DB 600's for fighter production, the He 111D did not enter large-scale production, the next major versions being the Jumo-powered He 111E and F. The latter employed the revised, straight-tapered wings originally evolved for the proposed commercial G model. Both E and F models also served in Spain, and after the Civil War the surviving He 111's became a part of the Spanish Air Force. Production of the variants so far mentioned had reached nearly a thousand by the outbreak of World War 2, but a new

model had also made its appearance. This was the He 111P, whose extensively glazed, restyled front section, with its offset ball turret in the extreme nose, became characteristic of all subsequent variants. It was built in comparatively small numbers, again because of the use of Daimler-Benz engines, but its Jumo-powered counterpart, the He 111H, became the most widely used series of all, well over five thousand being built before production ended in 1944. Reflecting their rough reception during the Battle of Britain, successive H and subsequent types appeared with progressive increases in defensive armament, the number of crew members being increased to five or six according to the number of guns. Although most extensively used in its intended role as a medium bomber, the He 111H carried a variety of operational loads during its service. The H-6 was particularly effective as a torpedo bomber, carrying two of these weapons usually, while other H sub-types became carriers for the Hs 293 glider bomb and the FZG-76 (V1) flying bomb. More bizarre variants included the H-8 fitted with balloon-cable cutters, and the He 111Z *Zwilling* (Twin) glider tug, a union of two H-6 airframes linked by a new centre-section supporting a fifth Jumo engine. The H-23 was an 8-seat paratroop transport. German production, of all versions, was well in excess of seven thousand. Licence-built He 111H-16's, designated C.2111, were built in Spain by CASA, and served with the

Spanish Air Force until well into the 1960s.

24 Avro Anson

Design of the Anson twin-engined coastal reconnaissance monoplane was based upon that of the Avro 652 commercial 6-seater, and was known as the Avro 652A. The military prototype (K 4771) was flown on 24 March 1935, and in the following summer Specification 18/35 was issued to cover the initial contract for one hundred and seventy-four Anson Mk I's for Coastal Command. The first Ansons were delivered to No 48 Squadron in March 1936. By the outbreak of war the RAF had seven hundred and sixty serviceable Anson I's, equipping ten squadrons of Coastal Command and sixteen of Bomber Command, and production was still continuing. Strictly, by then they were obsolescent, and from 1940 began to be replaced by Whitleys and imported American Hudsons, but some continued to serve in the general reconnaissance role until 1942, while others carried out air/sea rescue duty with Coastal Command squadrons over an even longer period. Almost from the outset, the Anson had also been envisaged as an aircrew trainer, and it was essentially the impetus given by the gigantic Empire Air Training Scheme of 1939 that led ultimately to the manufacture of eight thousand one hundred and thirty-eight Ansons in Britain by 1952 (including six thousand seven hundred and four Mk I's), and a further two thousand eight hundred and eighty-two under the super-

vision of Federal Aircraft Ltd in Canada. Canadian-built Ansons, differing principally in powerplant, comprised the Mk II (330 hp Jacobs L-6BM), and the Mks V and VI (both with 450 hp Pratt & Whitney R-985-AN 14B). As an interim measure, two hundred and twenty-three British-built Mks III (Jacobs) and IV (Wright Whirlwind) were supplied to Canada. Anson trainers subsequently served with all major Commonwealth air forces, as well as those of Egypt, Finland, Greece, Ireland and the U.S. Army. Anson I's later converted for ambulance or light transport duty included one hundred and four as Mk X's, ninety as Mk XI's and twenty as Mk XII's. An additional two hundred and twenty-one aircraft were built as Mk XII's from the outset. The Mks XI and XII both featured the taller cabin that also characterised the post-war Avro XIX civil transport version.

25 Ilyushin Il-4

The most widely used Soviet bomber of the war years, the Il-4 began its career under the design bureau designation TsKB-26 in 1935; its military or functional designation was DB-3, the letters indicating *Dalnii Bombardirovchtchik* or Long-Range Bomber. It was chosen for development, in preference to the contemporary DB-2 designed by Pavel Sukhoi, in its slightly modified TsKB-30 form, and delivery of production DB-3's began in 1937. The initial production DB-3, a manoeuvrable aeroplane despite its size and weight, was characterised by its squarish, blunt nose, and was powered by two 765 hp M-85 radial engines; 960 hp M-86 engines replaced these in later production batches. Armament consisted of single hand-operated 7·62 mm ShKAS machine-guns in nose and dorsal turrets, with a third gun firing down through a trap in the rear fuselage floor. Some aircraft of the original type saw service during World War 2, although by then the current version was the DB-3F (for *Forsirovanni* = boosted), design of which had started in 1938. This was at first powered by 950 hp M-87A engines and later by the more powerful M-88B, but the chief structural difference lay in the complete redesign of the nose section. This was now longer, more streamlined, well provided with windows, and instead of the DB-3's angular turret its gun was provided with a universal joint mounting. The DB-3F entered production after completing its acceptance trials in June 1939, and during the following year (when it was redesignated Il-4) large numbers were built. As a result of the war, strategic materials became in short supply, and deliveries of M-87A engines could not be maintained at an adequate rate. Further redesign therefore took place, in which several of the fuselage components, and later the outer wing panels, were manufactured from wood instead of metal; and by mid-1942 the M-88B engine was introduced as the standard powerplant. Output then increased steadily until 1944, when Il-4 production ceased. The bomber

served extensively throughout the war with both the Soviet Air Force and Soviet Navy, and it was a force of Il-4's from the latter service which carried out the first long-range attack by Soviet aircraft on Berlin on the night of 8 August 1941. Subsidiary duties included reconnaissance and glider training.

26 Martin 167 Maryland

The slim, twin-engined monoplane that the British services came to know as the Maryland was evolved in 1938 to enter a USAAC design competition ultimately won by the Douglas DB-7. One prototype of the Martin 167W was ordered by the U.S. Army as the XA-22, and this aircraft (NX 22076) made its first flight on 14 March 1939. No U.S. orders were forthcoming, but in 1939 the French Government placed total orders for two hundred and fifteen for the *Armée de l'Air*. These had the Martin export designation 167F and the French military designation 167A-3. The first 167F flew in August 1939, and deliveries began in October. Probably no more than one-third of those ordered were delivered to France, where they were in action against the German advance in the spring of 1940. After the fall of France several of the survivors were operated by the Vichy Air Force during 1940-41. At least five are known to have escaped to serve with the Royal Air Force, and delivery of a further seventy-six from the original French orders was also diverted to the RAF. These received the name Maryland Mk I, and almost all of them were employed by bomber and reconnaissance squadrons in the Middle East. A further one hundred and fifty, with British equipment and a different mark of Twin Wasp engine, were ordered by the British Purchasing Mission as the Maryland Mk II. The clean but unusually slender lines of the Martin 167 led *The Aeroplane* to remark, in September 1940, that it 'is nice as an aeroplane but a little cramped as a fighting machine'. Nevertheless, the Maryland was comparatively fast for a twin-engined machine, especially when relieved of the necessity to carry a bomb load, and made a useful reconnaissance type during the middle years of the war. A reconnaissance by RAF Marylands preceded the Fleet Air Arm's November 1940 assault on the Italian Fleet at Taranto, and in May 1941 a Maryland of the Fleet Air Arm (which received a few of the RAF machines) first brought the news of the movement of the *Bismarck* which led to the action in which the German warship was sunk. Seventy-two of the final batch of Maryland II's were re-allocated to serve with four squadrons of the South African Air Force.

27 **Bristol Blenheim**
Developed from the Bristol 142 *Britain First*, the Blenheim twin-engined medium bomber first appeared in production form as the short-nosed Blenheim Mk I, whose prototype (K 7033) first flew on 25 June 1936. By that time an initial contract had already been placed, and the first Blenheim I's were delivered in March 1937 to No 114 Squadron. One thousand two hundred and eighty Mk I's were built, and at the outbreak of World War 2 one thousand and seven of these were on RAF charge, including one hundred and forty-seven completed as Mk IF fighters with a ventral pack of four Browning guns. Most of the bombers were serving in the Middle and Far East, home squadrons of the RAF having already begun to re-equip with the long-nosed Mk IV bomber, one hundred and ninety-seven of which were on strength at 3 September 1939. From the eighty-first machine onward these were designated Blenheim IVL, the suffix indicating a longer range by virtue of additional wing fuel tanks. With Mercury XV engines replacing the 840 hp Mercury VIII's of the Blenheim I, the Mk IV was better armed and had a slightly improved performance over its predecessor. One thousand nine hundred and thirty Mk IV's were completed. By contrast, the performance of the final British variant, the Mk V, was disappointing. This version was redesigned to meet Specification B.6/40, and in 1941 one Mk VA day bomber prototype and one close-support Mk VB were built by Bristol. Rootes Securities Ltd built nine hundred and forty-two examples, mostly as the Mk VD (a 'tropical' version of the VA), but including a proportion of Mk VC dual-control trainers. Combat losses of the Mk VD were heavy, and it was quickly replaced by US Baltimores and

Venturas. During their career Blenheims served with every operational command of the RAF and in every theatre of the war. Pre-war exports included Blenheim I's for Finland, Rumania, Turkey and Yugoslavia. The Mk I was built under licence in Yugoslavia, and both the Mks I and IV in Finland. In Canada, Fairchild built six hundred and seventy-six Blenheims for the Royal Canadian Air Force, by whom they were designated Bolingbroke Mks I to IV.

28 Bristol Beaufighter

The Beaufighter was originally designed as a fighter, and the principal variants to serve in this capacity are described in the companion volume *Fighters, Attack and Training Aircraft 1939–45*. Its design was, however, based to a large extent upon the Beaufort torpedo bomber, and although the torpedo-carrying models were officially designated TF (Torpedo Fighter), it was considered more appropriate to include them in this volume for purposes of comparison with other types performing a similar function. The first torpedo-dropping experiments were made in 1942 with X 8065, a standard Beaufighter VIC (the Coastal Command version) adapted to carry a standard British or U.S. torpedo beneath the fuselage. Thereafter an experimental squadron was formed, which achieved its first combat success off Norway in April 1943. The so-called 'Torbeau' proved an effective torpedo bomber while retaining enough of its former performance to

carry out its other coastal duties of escort fighter and reconnaissance. Sixty Mk VI's on the production line were completed as ITF (Interim Torpedo Fighters), but two new variants soon began to appear. These were the TF Mk X torpedo bomber and the non-torpedo-carrying Mk XIC, both with 1,770 hp Hercules XVII engines. The TF Mk X, two thousand two hundred and five of which were built, had AI radar installed in a character-istic nose 'thimble' fairing, and a dorsal fin extension was introduced on later production batches. It could carry a heavier torpedo than the Mk VI (ITF), or could, alter-natively, be equipped with two 250 lb (113 kg) bombs and eight rocket projectiles beneath the wings. The Mk VI (ITF) aircraft were later re-engined and brought up to Mk X standard. Three hundred and sixty-four Beaufighter Mk 21's were built for the RAAF by the Government Aircraft Factories at Fishermen's Bend and Mascot, NSW. Except for Hercules XVIII engines and four 0·50 in wing guns in place of the six Brownings, these were generally similar to the RAF's Mk X. It was they upon whom their Japanese opponents bestowed the respectful nickname of 'Whispering Death'. In spite of its later designation, the Mk XIC was only an interim model pending large-scale delivery of the Mk X, and only one hundred and sixty-three were built.

29 Bristol Beaufort

The Type 152 proposals submitted in April 1936 were designed to meet two Air Ministry Specifications: M.15/35 for a torpedo bomber, and G.24/35 for a general reconnaissance aeroplane. Detail design work began in March 1937. The prototype (L 4441) first flew on 15 October 1938, powered by two 1,065 hp Bristol Taurus II radials in place of the Perseus originally planned. Specification 10/36 was framed to cover production aircraft, seventy-eight of which had been ordered in September 1936, and the Beaufort I entered production in 1939. Initially this was armed with one 0·303 in machine-gun in the port wing and two in the dorsal turret; later, a rear-firing gun was added in an off-set blister beneath the nose, and some aircraft also had twin K guns in the nose and two others in beam positions. Bristol built nine hundred and sixty-five Beaufort I's, first deliveries being made to No 22 Squadron, Coastal Command. In January 1940 a Beaufort from this unit came close to sinking the battle cruiser *Gneisenau* in Brest harbour on 6 April 1941, and Beauforts of No 86 Squadron played an important part in trying to prevent the 'Channel dash' by the *Gneisenau*, *Scharnhorst* and *Prinz Eugen* early in 1942. Other RAF Beaufort squadrons in the United Kingdom and Mediterranean included Nos 39, 42, 47, 203, 217, 415 and 489. They remained in service until replaced by torpedo-carrying Beaufighters in 1943, their duties including mine-laying. At the outset the Beaufort had also been chosen for production in Australia. In November 1940 one aircraft was flown with 1,200 hp

Pratt & Whitney R-1830-S1C3G Twin Wasp engines, becoming the prototype for four hundred and fifteen similarly powered Beaufort II's for the RAF. Many of these were completed, and others later converted, as operational trainers, with a dorsal turret faired over. Another Twin-Wasp engined prototype was flown in Australia in May 1941, and up to August 1944 seven hundred Beauforts were built there. These comprised fifty Mk V, thirty Mk VA, forty Mk VI, sixty Mk VII and five hundred and twenty Mk VIII. These differed chiefly in the engine variant or equipment fitted, though the enlarged fin introduced on the Mk VII later became standard on all Australian Beauforts. They served with the RAAF in the Solomons, Timor, New Guinea and several other Pacific battle areas. In November 1944 forty-six aircraft were converted into Mk IX troop transports. A Mk III was proposed, but not built, with Merlin XX engines and Beaufighter 'long-range' outer wing sections; one Mk IV was completed, with 1,750 hp Taurus engines.

30 De Havilland Mosquito

One of the outstandingly versatile aeroplanes of any era, the D.H.98 Mosquito was first conceived, in 1938, as a day bomber fast enough to outrun enemy fighters and thus carry no armament. Not until March 1940 was firm official interest shown in the design, fifty then being ordered. Three prototypes were built; the first and second of these

(W4050 and W4051) being completed in bomber and photo-reconnaissance configuration respectively. They flew on 25 November 1940 and 10 June 1941. The initial fifty aircraft included ten PR Mk 1 and ten B Mk IV, and the first operational Mosquito sortie was flown by an aircraft of the former batch on 20 September 1941. The B IV's entered service with No 105 Squadron in May 1942, and two hundred and seventy-three Mk IV's were eventually built. In addition to three de Havilland factories in the United Kingdom, contributions to overall Mosquito production were also made by Airspeed (one hundred and twenty-two), Percival (two hundred and forty-five) and Standard Motors (one hundred and sixty-five). De Havilland built altogether five thousand and seven Mosquitos, four thousand four hundred and forty-four of them during the war period. In addition, two hundred and eight (Mks 40–43) were built by de Havilland Australia, and one thousand one hundred and thirty-four (Mks VII, 20–22 and 24–27) by de Havilland Canada. Wartime Mosquito production totalled six thousand seven hundred and ten, with a further one thousand and seventy-one completed after VJ-day. Mosquitos quickly established a reputation for their excellent flying qualities, their unequalled talent for destroying pin-point targets, and for having easily the lowest loss rate of any aircraft in service with Bomber Command. Mosquito IV's originally equipped the Pathfinder

Force, which later employed also the high-altitude Mk IX and the second most numerous variant, the Mk XVI; and photo-reconnaissance counterparts of these three Marks constituted the principal wartime PR variants of the Mosquito. From early in 1944 the most popular Mosquito weapon was the 4,000 lb (1,814 kg) 'block-buster' bomb, carried in a specially bulged bomb bay retrospectively fitted to all Mks IX and XVI and several Mk IV's. About one thousand two hundred Mosquito XVI's were built, and were later flown with auxiliary pinion fuel tanks to increase their range. The NF Mk II, FB Mk VI and other fighter and fighter-bomber variants are described in the *Fighters, Attack and Training Aircraft 1939–45* volume.

31 **Junkers Ju 88**
The most adaptable German warplane of World War 2, and among the most widely used, the Ju 88 was evolved to a 1937 requirement issued by the RLM for a fast, well-armed multi-purpose aeroplane. The first prototype (D-AQEN) was flown on 21 December 1936, powered by two 1,000 hp DB 600A in-line engines. The second prototype was essentially similar, but in the third the powerplant was a pair of Jumo 211A engines, and the Jumo was to power the majority of Ju 88's subsequently built. The characteristic multi-panelled glazed nose section first appeared on the fourth prototype. A pre-series batch of Ju 88A-0's were completed during the summer of 1939, and delivery

of the first Ju 88A-1 production models began in September. The A series continued, with very few gaps, through to the A-17, and included variants for such specialised roles as dive bombing, anti-shipping strike, long range reconnaissance and conversion training. Probably the most common model was the A-4, which served both in Europe and North Africa. This was the first version to incorporate modifications resulting from operational experience gained during the Battle of Britain; it had extended-span wings, Jumo 211J engines, increased bomb load and defensive armament. Twenty Ju 88A-4's were supplied to Finland, and others to the *Regia Aeronautica*. The Ju 88B, evolved before the outbreak of war, followed a separate line of development to become the Ju 188, and the next major production model, chronologically, was the Ju 88C fighter series. The Ju 88D (over one thousand eight hundred built as D-1, D-2 and D-3) was a developed version of the A-4 for the strategic reconnaissance role. Next bomber series was the Ju 88S, powered by 1,700 hp BMW 801G radials (in the S-1), 1,810 hp BMW 801TJ's (S-2) or 1,750 hp Jumo 213E-1's (S-3). Apart from powerplant, the S sub-types were basically similar to one another, and differed from the earlier bombers in having a smaller, fully rounded glazed nose. They were less heavily armed, and carried a smaller bomb load, but performance compared with the A and D series was considerably better. The Ju 88T-1 and T-3 were

photo-reconnaissance counterparts of the S-1 and S-3. Production of bomber and reconnaissance variants of the Ju 88 totalled ten thousand seven hundred and seventy-four, just over 60 per cent of the overall total. Other major versions are dealt with in the *Fighters, Attack and Training Aircraft 1939–45* volume. Towards the end of the war many Ju 88 airframes ended their days rather ignominiously as the explosive-laden lower portion of *Mistel* composite attack weapons, carrying a Bf 109 or Fw 190 pick-a-back fashion to guide them on to their targets.

32 Douglas DB-7 series
Douglas submitted its Model 7A design in a 1938 U.S. Army competition for a twin-engined attack bomber, and was authorised to build prototypes for evaluation. The first appeared as the improved Model 7B, with 1,100 hp Twin Wasp engines and a tricycle undercarriage, first flying on 26 October 1939. First customer was France, which ordered one hundred in February 1939; the first U.S. orders, for one hundred and eighty-six A-20's and A-20A's, followed three months later. These, with the manufacturer's designation DB-7, had a narrower but deeper fuselage. The first DB-7 was flown on 17 August 1939, with 1,050 hp Twin Wasps. On 14 October French DB-7 orders were increased to two hundred and seventy, the second batch to have uprated engines; six days later a further hundred were ordered, designated DB-7A and having 1,600 hp

Wright Cyclones. Little more than a hundred DB-7's had been delivered before the fall of France in 1940, and the remainder were diverted to Britain. The DB-7's were initially named Boston I and II by the RAF, but later converted into Havoc I fighters; the DB-7A's became Havoc II. In February 1940 Britain ordered one hundred and fifty DB-7B's (not to be confused with the original Model 7B). These were similar to the DB-7A, but with seven 0·303 in guns instead of the latter version's six 7·5 mm guns. The RAF ultimately received seven hundred and eighty-one, named Boston III. Nine hundred and ninety-nine A-20B's were built for the U.S. Army. Features of the RAF's Boston III were incorporated into eight hundred and eight A-20C's for the USAAF. Of these, two hundred and two went to the RAF designated Boston IIIA. Next major U.S. variant was the A-20G, two thousand eight hundred and fifty being built with the 'solid' nose of the fighter variants and bomb-carrying capacity later increased to 4,000 lb (1,814 kg). Production batches of the A-20G varied in armament, and some carried a ventral fuel tank. The four hundred and twelve A-20H's were similar apart from their 1,700 hp Twin Wasp engines. A one-piece moulded transparent nose characterised the A-20J (four hundred and fifty built) and A-20K (four hundred and thirteen built), known in the RAF as the Boston IV and V. Overall production of the DB-7 'family', including the Havoc fighter models,

totalled seven thousand three hundred and eighty-five, and came to an end in September 1944. Almost half of this output went to the U.S.S.R., but USAAF and RAF variants served in all theatres of the war, undertaking a wide range of operational duties beyond those for which they were designed. Small quantities were employed by the U.S. Navy, and by the air forces of Brazil and Canada.

33 Douglas A-26 Invader

Although nowadays best known for its operational service in Korea, the Congo and Vietnam, the Douglas Invader's design was actually begun in January 1941, well before the U.S. entered World War 2. It was initiated as a successor to the Douglas A-20 Havoc, and in June 1941 the USAAF ordered three prototypes. The first of these was flown on 10 January 1942, but each was completed to a different configuration. The original XA-26 was an attack bomber, with a 3,000 lb (1,361 kg) internal bomb load, twin guns in its transparent nose section and two others in each of the dorsal and ventral turrets; the XA-26A, a night fighter, had a solid radar-carrying nose, four cannon in a ventral tray and four 0·50 in guns in the upper turret; while the XA-26B had a shorter nose mounting a single 75 mm cannon. In the initial production model, the A-26B, the armament was changed yet again (see caption on page 49), and the bomb load increased. Later production batches introduced R-2800-79 engines with water injection, boosting the power and performance at altitude, the number of nose guns was increased to eight, and additional gun-packs, rocket projectiles or 2,000 lb (907 kg) of bombs could be carried beneath the wings. To concentrate the fire-power even more, the dorsal guns could be locked forward and fired by the pilot. Five hundred and thirty-five water-injection A-26B's were built, following the initial eight hundred and twenty by Douglas's Long Beach and Tulsa factories. The Invader made its European operational debut in the autumn of 1944, and its first Pacific appearance early in 1945. The A-26C, which appeared in 1945, also saw limited service before the war ended. This had the twin-gun transparent 'bombardier' nose, but was otherwise similar to the B model. With the arrival of VJ-day, large numbers of Invader orders were cancelled, but even so, one thousand and ninety-one A-26C's were completed. In Europe alone, A-26 series aircraft flew over eleven thousand sorties and dropped more than eighteen thousand tons of bombs for the loss of sixty-seven aircraft in combat; curiously, despite their formidable firepower, they destroyed only seven enemy aircraft during this period. After the war, redesignated in the B-26 series after the Martin Marauder was withdrawn in 1958, they became a standard post-war USAF type, and the latest models continue to serve in Vietnam some twenty-five years after their first operational mission.

34 Martin Baltimore

The Baltimore was designed specifically to British requirements, to provide an improved successor to the Martin 167 operated by the RAF as the Maryland. It appeared as the Martin 187, the first production aircraft (there was no separate prototype) flying on 14 June 1941, some thirteen months after the RAF had placed an order for four hundred. These were built as Baltimore Mks I (fifty), II (one hundred) and III (two hundred and fifty), all being similarly powered and having four wing guns and one rearward-firing and four-downward-firing ventral guns. Only the dorsal armament distinguished them, the Mks I and II having single and twin Vickers K guns respectively, while the Mk III had a Boulton Paul four-gun turret. The Baltimore was given the USAAF designation A-30, although none served with the American forces. Lend-Lease supplies included two hundred and eighty-one Baltimore IIIA's (identical to the Mk III), two hundred and ninety-four Mk IV's and six hundred Mk V's, bringing overall manufacture to one thousand five hundred and seventy-five before production ended in May 1944. The Baltimore IV (illustrated) replaced the Boulton Paul turret by a twin-gun Martin turret, and the Baltimore V was similar except for the up-rated 1,700 hp R-2600-29 engines. The Baltimore, like the Maryland, served exclusively in the Middle East theatre, where it equipped several squadrons of the RAF from the spring of 1942 onward. Two squadrons of the South African Air Force were also equipped with them, and several were operational in the Balkans area, especially over Yugoslavia, with the *Stormo Baltimore* of the Italian Co-Belligerent Air Force in 1944-45. A few others were handed over to the Royal Navy for non-operational duties.

35 Martin B-26 Marauder

Finishing the war with a combat loss rate of less than 1 per cent, the Marauder more than vindicated its early reputation as a 'widow maker', which arose chiefly from the high accident rate created by inexperienced pilots handling an unfamiliar and unusually heavy aeroplane. As the Martin 179, its design was entered for a 1939 U.S. Army design competition and was rewarded by an immediate order for two hundred and one aircraft without the usual prototype preliminaries. The first B-26, flown on 25 November 1940, exhibited a modest armament, compared with later models, of only five defensive guns. Delivery to USAAC units began in 1941, in which year there also appeared the B-26A, with heavier calibre nose and tail guns, provision for extra fuel tanks in the bomb bay and for carrying a torpedo beneath the fuselage. One hundred and thirty-nine B-26A's were completed, making their operational debut from Australian bases in the spring of 1942. The B-26 also appeared in action from Alaskan and North African bases. Then followed the B-26B, with uprated engines and increased armament. Of the one thousand eight hundred and eighty-three built, all but the first six hundred and forty-one B-26B's also introduced a new, extended-span wing and taller tail. The B-26B made its operational debut in Europe in May 1943, subsequently becoming one of the hardest-worked Allied medium bombers in this theatre. One thousand two hundred and ten B-26C's were built, essentially similar to the later B models. These were succeeded by the B-26F (three hundred built), in which the wing incidence was increased with the purpose of improving take-off performance and reducing the accident rate. The final model was the B-26G, which differed only slightly from the F; nine hundred and fifty G models were completed, the last being delivered in March 1945. Of the overall U.S. production supplies to the RAF under Lend-Lease included fifty-two B-26A's (as Marauder I's), two hundred B-26F's (Marauder II) and one hundred and fifty B-26G's (Marauder III). Many other Marauders were completed for the USAAF as AT-23 or TB-26 trainers, and some for the U.S. Navy as JM-1's.

36 PZL P.37 Łoś (Elk)

This elegant Polish medium bomber was among the best of its type to appear in the 1930s, but lack of appreciation of its qualities by the Army authorities controlling aircraft procurement for the Polish Air Force denied it the commercial and operational successes that it deserved. The original design, by Jerzy Dabrowski, received approval from the Department of Aeronautics in October 1934, and was developed under the designation P.37. In August 1935 work began on two flying prototypes and a static test airframe, and the P.37/I flew late in June 1936 with two 873 hp Polish-built Bristol Pegasus XIIB engines. This prototype, and nine of the first ten similarly powered Łoś A production aircraft, had a single fin and rudder. The P.37/II prototype, and all other production Łoś bombers, had a twin-tail assembly. The P.37/II, which flew in April 1937, was prototype for the Łoś B, differing principally in its more powerful Pegasus XX engines and an ingenious cantilever main landing gear. Orders were placed for twenty more Łoś A's and one hundred and fifty Łoś B's, the majority to be delivered by 1 April 1939. Delivery of the Łoś B began in autumn 1938, when the existing Łoś A's were fitted with dual controls and transferred to operational conversion training with No 213 Squadron. The Army used devious means to denigrate the P.37's operational worth, cutting back military orders for the Łoś B in April 1939 when only a hundred had been completed. The P.37/II was refitted with several alternative engines, including the Gnome-Rhône 14N.1 of 970 hp and the 14N.20/21 of 1,050 hp, which were intended for use in the proposed Łoś C and Łoś D export models. Before the outbreak of war PZL had received encouraging orders from Bulgaria, Rumania, Turkey and Yugoslavia; and had good prospects of further sales or licences in Belgium, Denmark, Estonia and Greece. However, none of these aircraft were delivered, and the Polish Air Force itself had only some ninety Łoś bombers on charge when the war began. Of these, thirty-six were with Nos 211, 212, 216 and 217 Squadrons of the Tactical Air Force's Bomber Brigade which had been formed in the previous summer. In the second week of fighting nine more were acquired, but twenty-six of the forty-five operational machines were lost during the sixteen days before the U.S.S.R. invaded Poland from the east. The surviving aircraft, with twenty-seven others from Brzesc airfield, were withdrawn to Rumania, in whose colours they subsequently fought against Soviet forces. Variants included an abortive heavy fighter project with an eight-gun 'solid' nose, and the P.49/I Miś (Teddy Bear). The latter, incomplete when the war started, was the prototype for a more powerful and more heavily armed bomber version.

37   Mitsubishi Ki-21

The Ki-21 won an exacting design competition initiated by the Japanese Army Air Force early in 1936, and the first of five prototypes was completed in November of that year. With improved fields of fire for the defensive guns, and 850 hp Nakajima Ha-5-*Kai* engines replacing the Mitsubishi Kinsei Ha-6's of the first prototype, it was accepted for initial production as the Ki-21-Ia, or Type 97 heavy bomber. It entered JAAF service in 1937, and in 1938 Nakajima began to contribute to the production programme, delivering its first Ki-21 in August. The Model 1A was quickly succeeded by the Model 1B (Ki-21-Ib), into which were built modifications resulting from combat experience during the fighting with China. Increases were made in protective armour for the crew, defensive armament and the sizes of the flaps and bomb bay. The Model 1C (Ki-21-Ic) had increased fuel and an extra lateral gun. A wider-span tailplane was introduced on the Model 2A (Ki-21-IIa). Mitsubishi began the development of this late in 1939, replacing the former power-plant by 1,490 hp Ha-101 engines. The Ki-21 was a standard Army bomber at the time of Pearl Harbor, and was subsequently encountered in Burma, Hong Kong, India, Malaya, the Netherlands East Indies and the Philippines. Under the Allied code-naming system, the Ki-21 was known as 'Sally', although the name 'Gwen' was briefly allocated to the Model 2B (Ki-21-IIb) before it was recognised as a Ki-21 variant. The Model 2B was the final production variant of this now-obsolescent bomber, recognisable by the turret replacing the dorsal 'greenhouse' of the earlier models. With its appearance, many earlier Ki-21's were withdrawn either for training or for conversion to MC-21 transports. Shortly before the war ended, nine Ki-21's were made ready as assault transports at Kyushu, to transfer demolition troops to Okinawa, but only one

reached its target. Production came to an end in September 1944 after one thousand seven hundred and thirteen had been built by Mitsubishi, plus three hundred and fifty-one by Nakajima (up to February 1941). Just over five hundred transport counterparts of the Ki-21 were built by Mitsubishi, designated MC-20 in their civil form and Ki-57 (code-name 'Topsy') in military guise. Proposals for a Ki-21-III version were shelved in favour of the Ki-67.

38 Mitsubishi G4M

The G4M was evolved to a 'range-at-all-costs' specification, issued by the Japanese Navy in 1937 for a twin-engined medium bomber. Kiro Honjo, who led the design team, could only accomplish this by packing so much fuel into the wings that no armour protection could be provided for the fuel tanks or the crew. Then, after the prototype G4M1 had flown in October 1939, Mitsubishi were instructed to adapt the design for bomber escort duties, with increased armament and a crew of ten. Thirty G6M1's, as this version was known, had been built and service tested before the JNAF admitted their performance was inadequate and abandoned the project. The aircraft subsequently served as G6M1-K trainers and later still as G6M1-L2 troop transports. By the end of March 1941, however, fourteen more G4M1 bombers had been flown, and in April this version was accepted for service with the JNAF as the Model 11 land-based attack bomber. The G4M1 had a single 20 mm tail gun, with 7·7 mm guns in each of the nose, ventral and dorsal positions; powerplant was two 1,530 hp Mitsubishi Kasei 11 radials. The G4M1 was used by Japan in pre-war operations in south-east China, and by the time of her entry into World War 2 there were some one hundred and eighty G4M1's in service with the JNAF. They scored a number of early successes, but the 1,100 gallons (5,000 litres) of unprotected fuel in their tanks made them extremely vulnerable and the bomber soon became known to U.S. gunners as the 'one-shot lighter'. Three months after particularly heavy losses in the Solomons campaign of August 1942, Mitsubishi began work on the G4M2 Model 22. This had an improved armament, and 1,850 hp Kasei 21 engines with methanol injection; the fuel capacity was increased, but still the tanks remained unprotected. Nevertheless, the G4M2 became the major production model, appearing in five other versions: the G4M2a Model 24 (bulged bomb doors, Kasei 25 engines); G4M2b Model 25 (Kasei 27's); G4M2c Model 26 (total of two 20 mm and four 7·7 mm guns); G4M2d (for flight-testing the Ne-20 turbojet engine); and the G4M2e Model 24-J (four 20 mm guns and one 7·7 mm). Model 24-J's were later adapted as carriers for the Ohka suicide aircraft. Late in 1943, in the face of continuing heavy losses, Mitsubishi built sixty examples of the G4M3a Model 34 and G4M3b Model 36. These carried a reduced fuel load of 968 gallons (4,400 litres), in fully protected tanks, in a much-re-designed wing. Total production of G4M's (Allied code name 'Betty') amounted to two thousand four hundred and seventy-nine aircraft, many of which were converted to 20-seat troop transports towards the end of the war. Flight trials of a G4M3c Model 37, with exhaust-driven superchargers were partially completed before VJ-day; another project, the G4M4, was abandoned.

39 Mitsubishi Ki-67 Hiryu (Flying Dragon)

Design of the Ki-67, led by Dr Hisanojo Ozawa, began late in 1941 to a JAAF specification issued early that year. The first prototype was flown at the beginning of 1943, and by the end of that year fifteen Ki-67's had been completed. The Hiryu showed a considerable advancement over earlier Army bombers, not only in performance but in the degree of armour protection afforded to the crew members and the fuel installation. It was ordered into production in Model 1A form (Ki-67-Ia) early in 1944, and began to enter service during the summer. First combat appearance of the Ki-67 (code-named 'Peggy' by the Allies) was during the Battle of the Philippine Sea, where it was flown by Army crews but operated as a torpedo bomber under the direction of the Japanese Navy. The Model 1A was soon supplanted in production by the Model 1B (Ki-67-Ib), in which the former's flush-mounted beam guns were replaced by transparent blisters. By the end of the war

Mitsubishi had built six hundred and six Hiryus, while others had been completed by Kawasaki (ninety-one), Nippon Hikoki (twenty-nine) and the Army Air Arsenal (one). The majority of Ki-67's operated from Kyushu, and were encountered during the final year of the war in the Iwo Jima, Marianas and Okinawa battle areas, among others. Some became test-beds for the proposed Ki-67-II (two 2,500 hp Ha-214 engines), but this was still incomplete when the war ended. One development that did materialise was the Ki-109 'heavy' fighter. This replaced the originally proposed Ki-69 escort fighter version of the Hiryu, and the later Ki-112 project of 1943. Two Model 1B bombers were assigned early in 1944 to the Tachikawa Army Air Arsenal, where they were converted to mount a 75 mm Type 88 cannon in the nose, the only other armament being a 12·7 mm tail gun. Twenty of these 4-seat fighters were built, but Mitsubishi's inability to deliver any of the Ha-104ru turbo-supercharged engines intended for them caused them to be fitted with the same non-supercharged units as the bomber versions. With these they were unable to reach the combat altitude necessary to carry out the task for which they had been built – interception of the B-29 Superfortress bombers attacking Japan.

40 Nakajima Ki-49 Donryu

The first prototype Ki-49 was flown in August 1939, having been designed to a JAAF specification issued at the end of the preceding year. It was followed by a second prototype, each being powered by Nakajima Ha-5B engines. The Ki-49 had been evolved as a replacement for the Mitsubishi Ki-21, with the object of overcoming the slow speed and poor defensive armament of the latter; but the prototypes proved less than 20 mph (32 kmh) faster than the Ki-21, had a poor operational ceiling and were armed only with a single 20 mm cannon and two 7·92 mm machine-guns. Some improvement was made in subsequent prototypes, and in the Ki-49-I Model 1 which entered production in the late spring of 1940, by installing 1,250 hp Ha-41 engines. One hundred and twenty-nine Ki-49-I's were built at Ota, and the name Donryu was bestowed by the manufacturer, after the well-known Shinto shrine there. (A colloquial translation of Donryu is 'Dragon Swallower'.) In the Allied coding system the Ki-49 was known as 'Helen'. The Ki-49-IIa, the next production version, had three additional 7·92 mm guns; in the Ki-49-IIb all five machine-guns were of 12·7 mm calibre. Six hundred and forty-nine Ki-49-II's were built by Nakajima, fifty by Tachikawa and a small number by Mansyu. The parent company also completed six examples of a Ki-49-III, with 2,500 hp Ha-117 engines, but this version was not developed, and production of the Donryu ceased in December 1944. First operational appearance of the Ki-49-I was on 19 February 1942, when a force of them attacked Port Darwin in Australia from New

Guinea. The Ki-49-II, which entered service in the following September, was encountered in the China-Burma-India theatre, the Netherlands East Indies, Formosa and the Philippines. After the Leyte Island campaign, in which many were lost, they were extensively used for suicide attacks, though some were employed for mine detection and coastal patrol. A Ki-49, carrying Emperor Hirohito's envoy to Okinawa to sign the surrender agreement on 19-20 August 1945, made the last flight of the war by a JAAF aircraft. Such was the insistence on engine power and defensive armament that the Ki-49 inevitably suffered from having a small bomb load and inadequate range. Three Ki-58 fighter prototypes, based on the Ki-49-IIa, were built with five 20 mm and three 12·7 mm guns; and two Ki-49-III's were converted as formation leaders with the designation Ki-80.

41 Mitsubishi Ki-46

The Ki-46, in terms of aerodynamics and performance one of the best Japanese aircraft to serve during World War 2, was designed by Tomio Kubo to a JAAF requirement issued in December 1937. The specification was a rigorous one, for a fast, high altitude, long range, twin-engined reconnaissance aeroplane capable of speeds more than 50 mph (80 km/hr) faster than the latest western single-engined fighters. These demands were met by ingenious weight-saving and excellent streamlining, and the first prototype, powered by 875 hp Mitsubishi Ha-26-I engines, was flown in November 1939. The aircraft entered immediate production as the Ki-46-I, or Army Type 100 Model 1 Command Reconnaissance monoplane. The initial thirty-four aircraft were similarly powered, and were armed with a single 7·7 mm Type 89 machine-gun on a movable mounting in the rear cabin. They were used mostly for service trials and crew training, the main production version being the Ki-46-II Model 2, which first flew in March 1941. One thousand and ninety-three Model 2's were built, with 1,080 hp Ha-102 engines providing enhanced performance. Delivery of these began in July 1941, initially to JAAF units in Manchuria and China. The Ki-46 (code named 'Dinah' by the Allies) subsequently appeared in virtually every theatre of the Pacific war. A few Ki-46-II's were also used by the Japanese Navy, and others were converted in 1943 to Ki-46-II-Kai operational trainers, with a second, raised cockpit behind the pilot's cabin. In December 1942 two prototypes were flown of the Ki-46-III, and six hundred and nine Model 3's were completed. The Ki-46-IIIa featured a modified nose canopy, eliminating the former step in front of the pilot's cabin, carried additional fuel and dispensed with the dorsal gun. Four prototypes were also built in 1945 of the Ki-46-IVa, basically similar but with turbo-supercharged Ha-112-IIru engines, but no production was undertaken. The entire one thousand seven hundred and forty-two Ki-46's were built by Mitsubishi at Nagoya and, later, at Toyama. In 1944, however, a substantial quantity of Model 3's began to be converted to Ki-46-III-Kai fighters by the Army Aeronautical Research Institute at Tachikawa for Japanese home defence. Conversion involved a 'stepped' nose, broadly similar to the original one, housing two 20 mm Ho-5 cannon and, between the front and rear crew cabins, a 37 mm Ho-203 cannon fixed to fire forward and upward. The Ki-46-IIIb, of which a few were built for ground attack, was similar, but omitted the dorsal cannon. Projected fighter variants included the Ki-46-IIIc (twin Ho-5's) and Ki-46-IVb (two nose-mounted Ho-5's).

42 Yokosuka P1Y1 Ginga (Milky Way)

The Ginga, code-named 'Frances' by the Allies, was evolved to a Japanese Navy 15-Shi (1940) requirement for a land-based bomber and dive bomber, though the first of several prototypes was not flown until early 1943. Designated Y-20, it was a handsome, well-built aeroplane with retractable under-wing air brakes. With its construction simplified and additional armour protection for the crew, the bomber was accepted for the JNAF as the P1Y1 Model 11. Production was undertaken by the Nakajima factories at Koizumi and Fukushima, which had built nine hundred and six Ginga bombers by the end of the war; delivery to combat units began in spring 1944. The Ginga was employed chiefly from land bases in Japan, especially from the island of Kyushu. In place of the usual single dorsal gun, some aircraft had a turret mounting twin 12·7 mm or 20 mm guns. Despite excellent flying qualities, the Ginga's operational career was restricted by the lack of skilled production staff, efficient pilots and fuel. Difficulties were also encountered with the Homare engines, which had been installed at the direction of the Navy. At Okinawa, many Gingas were employed as suicide aircraft. Kawanishi, invited to develop a night-fighter version of the Ginga, decided to replace the troublesome Homare with the more reliable Mitsubishi Kasei 25 radial of 1,850 hp. Kawanishi proposed two new variants – the P1Y2 bomber and the P1Y2-S night fighter – but preference was given to the latter type. A prototype was flown in June 1944, and ninety-six production aircraft, designated P1Y2-S Model 26 Kyokko (Aurora), were built. They carried elementary AI radar, and were armed with three 20 mm cannon, one on a movable mounting in the rear cabin and the other pair fixed to fire forward and upward from amidships. Despite Japan's urgent need of a strong home defence, the P1Y2-S had still only reached trials units when the war ended. The only operational night fighters were a few P1Y1-S conversions of Nakajima-built bombers. Some of these had a hand-operated dorsal turret with two 20 mm cannon, but none carried radar. One Ginga was used in 1945 to flight-test the Ne-20 turbojet engine. A further night fighter, P1Y3-S with 1,990 hp Homare engines, was projected but not built; and another proposed variant, the Ginga-Kai, was to have acted as parent aircraft for the Model 22 version of the Ohka suicide aircraft.

43 Heinkel He 177 Greif (Griffin)

The fact that the He 177 was the only German long-range strategic bomber to go into series production during World War 2 was doubtless due chiefly to the official indecision and political interference with its development that gave little chance of its initial design faults being satisfactorily overcome before it was pressed into service. Had it been permitted a natural and uninterrupted development, its story might have been very different, for it was basically a conventional design in all but one respect. This was the radical decision to employ pairs of coupled engines, each pair in a single nacelle, driving a single propeller. It was designed to a 1938 specification for a dual-purpose heavy bomber and anti-shipping aircraft, and was, unbelievably, required to be stressed for dive bombing. The first prototype, flown on 19 November 1939, just managed to keep within the overall weight limits of the specification, but service variants of the He 177 became progressively heavier. More ominous, however, was the curtailment of the first flight due to engine overheating, which was to plague the He 177 throughout its career. Eight prototypes were completed,

followed by thirty-five pre-production He 177A-0's built by Arado and Heinkel and one hundred and thirty Arado-built He 177A-1's. The early aircraft in this batch were used for further trials, and after a brief and unhappy operational debut the remainder were also withdrawn from service. From late 1942 they were replaced by one hundred and seventy Heinkel-built A-3's and eight hundred and twenty-six A-5's, which had longer fuselages and repositioned engine nacelles. Main combat area of these models was the Eastern Front, where the bomber's use also for ground-attack produced some interesting variations in armament. Other He 177A's were employed as transports, and certain variants were equipped to carry Hs 293 or FX 1400 missiles externally. A few A-6's were built, but by now attention was being diverted to developing the *Greif* with four separately mounted engines. When the German forces evacuated Paris the prototype He 274A (formerly the He 177A-4) was still awaiting its first flight at the Farman factory at Suresnes. One He 177A-3 airframe became the four-engined He 277, to which Heinkel gave the false designation He 177B to overcome official disapproval of the re-engined design. This flew late in 1943 with four 1,730 hp DB 603A engines, followed by two more prototypes and a small production batch, but these did not enter squadron service.

44 Curtiss C-46 Commando

Designed by Curtiss-Wright in 1936 as a 36-seat commercial airliner designated CW-20, the prototype of this capacious transport (NX 19436) first flew on 26 March 1940. It was evaluated by the U.S. Army, under the designation C-55, but was then restored to civil standard and purchased by BOAC, who named it *St Louis* and operated it as a 24-seater between Gibraltar and Malta and on longer routes. The USAAF ordered an initial twenty-five, further modified and having 2,000 hp Pratt & Whitney R-2800-43 Twin Wasp engines, for service as C-46 troop and freight transports. Originally named Condor III, the C-46 was later renamed Commando, and was produced in substantial numbers for the USAAF and U.S. Navy. The two major production models were the C-46A (one thousand four hundred and ninety-one built) and C-46D (one thousand four hundred and ten), the former having a single, large loading door while the latter had double freight doors and a remodelled nose section. The B, C, G, H, K and L variants were experimental models that did not go into production, the other Army models being the single-door C-46E (seventeen built) and double-door C-46F (two hundred and thirty-four built). These were counterparts to the A and D models, with R-2800-75 instead of -51 engines. One hundred and sixty R5C-1's (corresponding to the C-46A) were also built for the U.S. Marine Corps, with whom they performed invaluable supply and casualty evacuation duties. The Army aircraft, employed predominantly in the Far East, became

famous for their round-the-clock flights across the Himalayas to keep open the supply routes between Burma and China. They first appeared in Europe in March 1945, when they were used to drop paratroops during the Rhine crossing. Compared with the civil prototype, the military Commando could airlift up to 40 troops, 33 stretcher cases or a 10,000 lb (4,536 kg) payload of freight or military equipment.

45 Douglas C-47 Skytrain series

First Douglas Commercial transports to be acquired by the U.S. services were a number of DC-2's (Army C-32A and C-34, Navy R2D-1), followed by thirty-five C-39's with DC-2 fuselages and the DC-3's tail surfaces and outer wing panels. The principal wartime versions of the DC-3 were the Twin Wasp-engined C-47 Skytrain, C-53 Skytrooper and the Navy R4D series, differing in minor detail only, except for their function. The first nine hundred and fifty-three C-47's were troop or cargo transports; they were followed in 1942 by four thousand nine hundred and ninety-one C-47A's, and from 1943 by three thousand one hundred and eight C-47B's, all by Douglas. One hundred and thirty-three TC-47B's were also built, for training duties. The Skytrooper, as its name implied, was specifically a troop transport, of which Douglas produced one hundred and ninety-three C-53's, eight C-53B's, seventeen C-53C's and one hundred and fifty-nine

C-53D's from 1941 to 1943. Seventeen C-117A VIP transports were delivered in 1945. Commercial airline DST's (Douglas Sleeper Transports) or DC-3's impressed for war service included thirty-six with designations C-48 to C-48C, one hundred and thirty-eight C-49 to C-49K, fourteen C-50 to C-50D, one C-51, five C-52 to C-52C, two C-68 and four C-84. The Sky-trooper preceded the C-47 into service (October 1941), despite its higher designation number; the first Skytrains were delivered in January 1942. More than one thousand two hundred were supplied under Lend-Lease to the RAF, by whom they were known as Dakota Mks I to IV. They first entered service with No 31 Squadron in Burma in June 1942. Additional roles included casualty evacuation and glider towing. Total wartime production of military DC-3's, which ended in August 1945, amounted to ten thousand one hundred and twenty-three, mostly built by Douglas. Nor was this all: in addition to about seven hundred supplied to the U.S.S.R. under Lend-Lease, the Soviet engineer Boris Lisunov spent some time at Douglas prior to initiating pro-duction of a Soviet-built version known as the Li-2 (formerly PS-84). Some two thousand were built in the U.S.S.R., including some with a gun turret just above and behind the crew cabin. Licence production was also undertaken in Japan, where Showa built three hundred and eighty L2D2's and L2D3's for the JNAF (code-named 'Tabby' by the

Allies) and Nakajima completed a further seventy.

46 Consolidated PBY Catalina

First flown as the XP3Y-1 on 21 March 1935, the Consolidated Model 28 was the first U.S. military flying boat with cantilever wings. Sixty were ordered as PBY-1's in 1935, deliveries (to Squadron VP-11F) beginning in October 1936. Fifty PBY-2's followed in 1937-38, and in the latter year three PBY-3's and a manufacturing licence were sold to the U.S.S.R. The Soviet version, designated GST, was powered by M-62 engines. Orders for the U.S. Navy continued with sixty-six PBY-3's and thirty-three PBY-4's, the latter introducing the prominent lateral observation blisters that characterised most subsequent versions. The RAF received one Model 28-5 for evalu-ation in July 1939, resulting in an order for fifty aircraft similar to the U.S. Navy's PBY-5. The RAF name Catalina was subsequently adopted for the PBY's in USN service. During 1940 the RAF doubled its original order, and others were ordered by Australia (eighteen), Canada (fifty), France (thirty) and the Netherlands East Indies (thirty-six). Of the U.S. Navy's original order for two hundred PBY-5's, the final thirty-three were completed as PBY-5A amphibians, and an additional one hundred and thirty-four were ordered to -5A standard. Twelve later became RAF Catalina III's, and twelve more were included in the NEI contract. Seven hundred and fifty-three PBY-5's were built, and seven hundred and ninety-four PBY-5A's, fifty-six of the latter for the USAF as OA-10's. Lend-Lease supplies to Britain included two hundred and twenty-five PBY-5B's (Catalina IA) and ninety-seven Catalina IVA's with ASV radar. Production continued with the tall-finned Naval Aircraft Factory PBN-1 Nomad (one hundred and fifty-six, most of which went to the U.S.S.R.) and the similar PBY-6A amphibian (two hundred and thirty-five, including seventy-five Army OA-10B's and forty-eight for the U.S.S.R.). Canadian Vickers-built amphibians went to the USAAF (two hundred and thirty OA-10A's) and RCAF (one hundred and forty-nine Cansos). Boeing (Canada) production included two hundred and forty PB2B-1's (mostly as RAF Catalina IVB's), seventeen RCAF Catalinas, fifty tall-finned PB2B-2's (RAF Catalina VI) and fifty-five RCAF Cansos. Total U.S./Canadian production of PBY models was three thousand two hundred and ninety, to which were added several hundred GST's built in the U.S.S.R.

47 Saab-18

The Saab-18 originated, under the project designation L 11, as a twin-engined recconaissance aircraft, two prototypes being ordered in November 1939 and February 1940. By the time the first of these flew on 19 June 1942 changing tactical requirements had caused it to be developed primarily as a light day bomber and dive bomber. In general configuration it closely resembled the Dornier Do 215 bomber, except that the crew cabin was offset to port to improve the pilot's downward vision. With 1,065 hp Twin Wasp engines, the prototype had been somewhat underpowered; nevertheless, in July 1942 production was started of an initial batch of sixty aircraft with these engines, and these began to enter *Flygvapnet* service in June 1944 in B 18A bomber and S 18A reconnaissance forms. On 10 June 1944 the prototype was flown of the B 18B, powered by two of the 1,475 hp Daimler Benz DB 605B in-line engines which by then were being licence-built in Sweden for the Saab-21 fighter. The production B 18B's, one hundred and twenty of which were completed, did not enter service until after the war (1946). They had a maximum internal bomb load of 3,307 lb (1,500 kg), a fixed armament of one 7·9 mm and two 13·2 mm guns, ejection seats for the pilot and navigator, and provision for carrying rocket projectiles beneath the wings. The final production version was the T 18B, whose prototype was flown on 7 July 1945; sixty-two were built. Originally intended as a torpedo-bomber, the T 18B served finally in the attack role, carrying a two-man crew and armed with one 57 mm Bofors gun and two 20 mm cannon. This version remained in service until 1956.

48 Dornier Do 217

A substantial number of Do 217 prototypes were built, the first of them flying in August 1938 and generally resembling a scaled-up Do 215B. All of the first six incorporated a novel four-leaf air brake, opening umbrella-style in operation and forming an extension of the rear fuselage when retracted. This feature proved troublesome to operate and was discarded on later models. First major series was the Do 217E, which entered production in 1941 following service trials with a small pre-series batch of Do 217A-o's in the preceding year. Numerous E sub-types appeared, powered by various models of the BMW 801 radial engine and differing in armament and other equipment. The Do 217E-5 carried additional radio gear for launching and guiding two underwing Hs 293 missiles. Many E-2's later became Do 217J night fighters. The next bomber series, with a redesigned and even more bulbous nose than its predecessors, was the Do 217K (1,700 hp BMW 801D). The K-2 and K-3 sub-types could carry special anti-shipping weapons beneath extended wings of 81 ft 4⅜ in (24·80 m) span. In-line engines – 1,750 hp DB 603A's – appeared in the Do 217M series, many of which were also converted later for night fighting as the Do 217N. Final production model, a reconnaissance version, was the Do 217P (also with DB 603A's), but only six of these were built. The Do 217W (or Do 216) twin-float torpedo bomber project remained uncompleted, and only prototypes were completed of the much-developed Do 317. Total output of Do 217 variants reached one thousand seven hundred and

thirty, all except three hundred and sixty-four of these being bomber models. The Do 217 night fighters are described in the *Fighters, Attack and Training Aircraft 1939–45* volume.

49   Dornier Do 17 and Do 215

The Do 17 was evolved originally as a 6-passenger, high-speed mailplane for Deutsche Luft hansa, the Do 17V1 first prototype making its maiden flight in the autumn of 1934. Three single-finned prototypes were built for DLH, but the extreme slimness of the aeroplane was its commercial undoing, the narrow fuselage demanding extraordinary agility by passengers in order to reach their seats. However, the RLM decided to evaluate the design in its efforts to procure a new medium bomber for the *Luftwaffe*. Further prototypes were ordered, the first of them (Do 17V4) setting the future design pattern by having twin fins and rudders. The specially stripped Do 17V8, with boosted engines, created a considerable stir at the Zürich International Military Aircraft Competition in July 1937, when its performance clearly outshone even the best of the single-seat fighters being displayed. By this time two production versions of the aircraft were already in *Luftwaffe* squadron service, and in 1938 joined the Condor Legion in the Spanish Civil War. These were the Do 17E-1 bomber, with 750 hp BMW VI engines and a 1,764 lb (800 kg) bomb load, and its reconnaissance-bomber counterpart, the Do 17F-1. Impressed by the V8's performance at Zürich, the Yugoslav Government ordered twenty of an export version, designated Do 17K and powered by 986 hp Gnome-Rhône 14N radials, which improved both speed and range. This model was later licence-built in Yugoslavia, and when Germany invaded the country in April 1941 seventy were in service; the few that survived the fighting were allocated to the Croatian Air Force after the Nazi occupation. To maintain the Do 17's performance in relation to contemporary fighters, two new production models appeared with supercharged engines. These were the Do 17M (900 hp Bramo 323A) and Do 17P series (865 hp BMW 132N), otherwise generally corresponding to the E and F models. Two experimental series, the Do 17R and Do 17S, between them gave rise to the Do 17U, a pathfinder bomber with DB 600A engines, and then to the Do 17Z. The latter, with Bramo 323A or 1,000 hp Bramo 323P's, featured a more angular, bulbous front fuselage, and over five hundred Z models were built for bombing, reconnaissance and training. Two of the pre-production Do 17Z-0's, redesignated Do 215V1 and V2, became foreign demonstrators with Bramo and Gnome-Rhône engines respectively. The only foreign order received was from Sweden, for eighteen Do 215A-1's with DB 601A engines, but these were taken over by the *Luftwaffe* before delivery. They were followed by one hundred and one Do 215B's, most of which were similar except for the B-5, a night fighter/intruder version with a six-gun 'solid' nose. Development

subsequently continued as the Do 217, described separately.

50 Armstrong Whitworth Whitley

Oldest of the three standard RAF twin-engined bombers at the outbreak of World War 2, the Whitley was designed to Specification B.3/34, and the first prototype (K 4586) was flown on 17 March 1936. Thirty-four Mk I Whitleys were built, powered by 795 hp Armstrong Siddeley Tiger IX radial engines, and the first deliveries were made to No 10 Squadron in March 1937. Late-production Mk I's introduced dihedral on the wings, which became standard for all subsequent machines. The forty-six Mk II's were followed by eighty Mk III's with 920 hp Tiger VIII engines and a retractable ventral turret aft of the wing trailing-edge. A change was made to in-line engines in the Mks IV and IVA, thirty-three and seven of which were completed with 1,030 hp Merlin IV and 1,145 hp Merlin X engines respectively. Merlin X's were also adopted for the main wartime version, the Mk V, of which one thousand four hundred and sixty-six were produced. This was redesigned with a longer fuselage and tail fins of a modified shape. One hundred and forty-six Whitley VII's were produced for general reconnaissance work with Coastal Command, having increased range and carrying ASV radar for anti-shipping patrols. A number of Mk V's were later converted to Mk VII standard. Strictly speaking, the Whitley was obsolete as a bomber by the outbreak of war, when the RAF had two hundred and seven (mostly Mks I to IV) on charge; and its first operational missions were leaflet-dropping and security patrols. However, in company with Hampdens, Whitleys made the first bombing raid of the war on German soil on 19-20 March 1940, and in June 1940 became the first British bombers to attack a target in Italy. Their front-line career ended late in 1942, when even the reconnaissance versions were withdrawn, but they continued to serve for the remainder of the war in the valuable, if less glamorous, roles of troop and freight transport and glider tug. Fifteen Whitley V's were converted for freighter duties with BOAC in the spring of 1942, but (except for one casualty) were returned to the RAF by 1943.

51 Handley Page Hampden

Following the Whitley and Wellington, the Hampden was the third of Britain's trio of twin-engined medium bombers to enter service, two hundred and twenty-six being on RAF strength on 3 September 1939, serving with ten squadrons. Designed to the same Specification (B.9/32) as the Wellington, the first of the two Hampden prototypes (K 4240) flew for the first time on 21 June 1936. An initial order, for one hundred and eighty Hampden Mk I's to Specification 30/36, followed two months later, and these began to be delivered from September 1938, the first recipient being No 49 Squadron. In production Hampdens the rather ugly square-

cut nose section was replaced by a curved Perspex moulding, the rear gun installations were modified and Pegasus XVIII's replaced the original Pegasus P.E.5S(a) engines. Even with these improvements, the Hampden was a disappointment operationally, the field of fire being very limited and the extremely narrow fuselage produced excessive fatigue for the 4-man crew. Later attempts to mitigate the bomber's defensive shortcomings by fitting twin guns in each of the rearward-firing positions improved the situation only marginally. Nevertheless, Hampdens continued in operational service with Bomber Command, principally on night bombing raids or minelaying, until September 1942, and many of them continued in service as torpedo bombers or reconnaissance aircraft with Coastal Command for a year or more after this. During their service Hampdens took part in the first bombing raids on Berlin and in the first of the 1,000-bomber raids on Cologne. One thousand two hundred and seventy Hampdens were built in the United Kingdom by Handley Page (five hundred) and English Electric (seven hundred and seventy). In Canada, Canadian Associated Aircraft Ltd also completed one hundred and sixty in 1940-41. Two Hampdens were re-engined with 1,000 hp Wright GR-1820-G105A Cyclones as prototypes for a Mk II version, but this did not go into production. Concurrently with the first RAF order, however, a contract had also been placed for one hundred of a variant with 1,000 hp Napier Dagger in-line engines, named Hereford; this order was later increased to one hundred and fifty. These were built by Short Bros & Harland, but due to powerplant problems, many of these were later re-engined to become Hampdens. Those that remained as Herefords served with operational training units only.

52 **Fiat B.R.20 Cicogna (Stork)**
The B.R.20 (indicating *Bombardamento Rosatelli*, after its designer) was evolved in 1935 to provide the *Regia Aeronautica* with a fast, well-armed light bomber. The prototype's first flight, on 10 February 1936, was soon followed by the initial production B.R.20, with 1,000 hp Fiat A.80 RC 41 engines and various detail modifications. The first of these entered service with the 13° *Stormo Bombardamento Terrestre* in September 1936. Before the outbreak of World War 2 Fiat also built two B.R.20L, these being demilitarised models for international competitions and record flights. From the summer of 1937, B.R.20 bombers became engaged in the Spanish Civil War, and in June 1940 this type equipped four bomber *Stormi*, some two hundred and fifty having been built up to that time. Meanwhile, late in 1939 the prototype had been flown of the B.R.20M (for *Modificato*), an improved version characterised chiefly by its somewhat longer fuselage, better-contoured nose section and strengthened wings. About sixty of these were in service in June 1940, and series production continued until summer 1942, at which time five hundred and eighty had been completed. The majority of these were built as B.R.20M's; at least a hundred were B.R.20's, but many of these aircraft were later brought up to B.R.20M standard. They were used regularly during the early part of the war for bombing duties in the Mediterranean area, the Eastern Front, and, briefly, with the *Corpo Aereo Italiano* based in Belgium for attacks on the United Kingdom. By the end of 1942, when they began to be replaced by later types, their main duties were coastal reconnaissance and convoy patrol, and many others were employed as operational trainers. Late in 1940 Fiat flight-tested the first prototype of a much redesigned model designated B.R.20*bis*, and a second was flown in 1942. This version had increased armament and bomb load, installed in a considerably refined fuselage with a nose section reminiscent of the Heinkel He 111 and He 115. The use of 1,250 hp Fiat A.82 RC 32 engines gave a marked increase in performance, but only a dozen or so of this model appear to have reached squadron service. In 1938 eighty-five B.R.20's were supplied to Japan, where they were used by the JAAF as an interim type in China pending quantity deliveries of the Mitsubishi Ki-21.

53 **North American B-25 Mitchell**
North American Aviation was awarded an immediate production contract for its NA-62 design, without the usual preliminary prototypes, and the first B-25 was

flown on 19 August 1940. By the end of the year twenty-four had been delivered, all except the first nine having the gull-winged appearance that was a characteristic of the bomber. They were followed in 1941 by forty B-25A's, then by one hundred and nineteen B-25's with dorsal and ventral gun turrets. First operational unit was the 17th Bombardment Group, which began to receive its B-25's in 1941. Production continued with one thousand six hundred and nineteen B-25C's and two thousand two hundred and ninety B-25D's from early 1942, and in April that year B-25B's flying off the USS *Hornet* made their epic raid on Tokyo. The B-25E and F were experimental models, production continuing with the B-25G, which carried two 0·50 in guns alongside a 75 mm cannon in a new 'solid' nose. Four hundred and five B-25G's were built, and a hundred and seventy-five earlier Mitchells were modified to carry a total of ten 0·50 in guns. An even more heavily armed 'gunship' was the B-25H, one thousand of which were produced with the 75 mm nose cannon and fourteen 0·50 in guns; this entered operational service in February 1944, joining the earlier multi-gunned Mitchells on anti-shipping strikes in the Pacific battle areas. Final production model, the B-25J (four thousand three hundred and eighteen built), reverted to the standard bomber nose, but retained the forward placing of the dorsal turret introduced on the H model. Mitchells in U.S. service operated predominantly in the Pacific war

zone, but large numbers were supplied elsewhere during the war. Two hundred and forty-eight B-25H's and four hundred and fifty-eight B-25J's were transferred to the U.S. Navy from 1943 as PBJ-1H's and -1J's, most being operated by Marine Corps squadrons. Eight hundred and seventy Mitchells of various models were supplied to the U.S.S.R. under Lend-Lease; twenty-three Mitchell I's (B-26B) and five hundred and thirty-eight Mitchell II's (B-25C and D) were received by the RAF; and others were supplied to Brazil (twenty-nine), China (one hundred and thirty-one) and the Netherlands (two hundred and forty-nine).

54 Lockheed Hudson

The Hudson was evolved at short notice, in 1938, to meet a British requirement for a coastal reconnaissance aircraft to supplement the Anson. Essentially, it was a militarised version of the Model 14 commercial airliner that had flown in July 1937, and an initial RAF order was placed for two hundred. The first of these was flown on 10 December 1938; deliveries of Hudson I's to Britain began in February 1939, the first recipient being No 224 Squadron. On arrival, many were fitted with twin-gun Boulton Paul turrets. On the outbreak of war the RAF had seventy-eight Hudsons on strength, and on 8 October 1939 one of them destroyed the first German aircraft to fall to RAF guns in the war. Lockheed supplied three hundred and fifty Hudson I's and twenty

similar Hudson II's before introducing the Mk III, with more
powerful Cyclone engines and
ventral and beam guns. Four
hundred and twenty-eight of this
version were ordered. The only
other direct purchases were three
hundred and nine Hudson V's with
1,200 hp Twin Wasp engines. Many
other Hudson's reached the RAF
under Lend-Lease, however. These
included three hundred and eighty-
two Cyclone-engined Mk IIIA's,
and thirty Mk IV's and four
hundred and fifty Mk VI's with
Twin Wasp engines. In 1941 the
Hudson was given USAAF designations: A-28 for the Twin Wasp
version and A-29 for the models with
Cyclone engines. Eighty-two A-28's
and four hundred and eighteen
A-29's went to the USAAF, except
for twenty A-28's that were transferred to the U.S. Navy with the
designation PBO-1. In service with
Squadron VP-82, one of these became the first U.S. aircraft of the war
to destroy a German submarine.
The Hudson continued in front-line
service with Coastal Command until
1943-44, but undertook a variety of
wartime duties that included agent-
dropping, transport and operational
training.

55 Lockheed Ventura

As the Hudson was evolved from the
commercial Lockheed Model 14, so
was the Ventura a militarised form
of the larger Model 18, also insti-
gated at the request of the British
Purchasing Commission in 1940.
The initial RAF contracts were for
six hundred and seventy-five aircraft,
of which the first one hundred and
eighty-eight were delivered from
summer 1942 as Ventura Mk I's,
following the first flight on 31 July
1941. They entered service with No
21 Squadron of Bomber Command
in October 1942 and made their
first operational sorties early in the
following month. The Ventura II
and Lend-Lease IIA which followed
had a different variant of Double
Wasp engines, an increased bomb
load of 3,000 lb (1,361 kg) and two
additional guns in the fuselage. However, the Ventura was less successful
in daylight operations than had been
hoped, and deliveries were halted
after about three hundred had been
delivered. The remaining IIA's were
acquired by the USAAF as B-34's,
and more than three hundred others
from previous RAF contracts became B-34A Lexington bombers or
B-34B navigation trainers with the
USAAF. The proposed Ventura III
(B-37) with Wright Cyclone engines
was cancelled after delivery of only
eighteen of the U.S. Army's order
for five hundred and fifty, and subsequent production concentrated
upon the PV-1 model for the U.S.
Navy, ordered in September 1942.
This model had R-2800-31 Double
Wasps, a 'solid' nose, six defensive
guns, provision for external drop
tanks and the ability to carry depth
charges or a torpedo as an alternative
to bombs. One thousand six hundred
PV-1's were built, three hundred
and fifty-eight of which went to RAF
Coastal Command and several
Commonwealth air forces as
Ventura GR Mk V's. Twenty-seven
of the Ventura II's originally

intended for Britain were acquired by the U.S. Navy and designated PV-3 (PV-2 being the designation already allotted to a Ventura development known as the Harpoon).

Lend-Lease deliveries included ten Mk IA and seventeen Mk II. Twenty aircraft corresponding to the American C-56B version were supplied to the Royal Netherlands Indies Army Air Corps.

56 Lockheed Lodestar

The pre-war Model 18 Lodestar commercial transport was selected by the U.S. Army for wartime production, three hundred and twenty-five being built as standard Army and Navy paratroop transports with the designation C-60A. A proposed freighter version with large cargo-loading doors was to have been built in even larger numbers, but this contract was cancelled. However, a variety of assorted civil Model 18's were acquired for war service under several separate designations. Those in USAAF service included thirty-six C-56 to C-56E; thirteen C-57 and seven C-57A; ten C-59; thirty-six C-60; and one C-66. The U.S. Navy designations R50-1, -2, -5 and -6 correspond to the USAAF's C-56, C-59, C-60 and C-60A, while the R5O-3 and -4 were 4-seat and 7-seat executive transports respectively. Many of the impressed commercial Model 18's were returned to their former owners during 1943-44, very few remaining in service beyond this date. Although not in service in great numbers, the Lodestar performed a wide range of duties that included troop and cargo transport, casualty evacuation and glider training. More than two dozen civil Lodestars were also impressed into service with the RAF, to whom

57 Armstrong Whitworth Albemarle

The A.W.41 Albemarle was designed by Armstrong Whitworth to Air Ministry Specification B.18/38, for a twin-engined medium bomber of mixed wood and metal construction that could be contracted extensively to firms outside the aircraft industry. Two prototypes were completed by Armstrong Whitworth, and the first flight was made by the second of these (P 1361) on 20 March 1930. Completion of the entire production run of six hundred aircraft was entrusted to A. W. Hawkesley Ltd at Gloucester, but only the first thirty-two (designated Mk I Series 1) were completed as bombers. For this role they were to have had a 6-man crew, including two gunners to man the four-gun dorsal turret and the retractable 'dustbin'-type, two-gun ventral turret; the dorsal turret was offset slightly to port to simplify access to the rear fuselage. The Albemarle, although it also had a fixed, shock-absorbing tailwheel, was the first British military aircraft with a retractable nosewheel undercarriage to enter service. The first production aircraft was completed in December 1941, but the Albemarle never served in its intended role, and these thirty-two aircraft were instead converted for transport duties. Deliveries began to No 295 Squadron at Harwell in January 1943. Subsequent Albemarles were designated ST (Special Transport) or GT (General Transport), and were completed as follows: ninety-nine ST Mk I, sixty-nine GT Mk I, ninety-nine ST Mk II, forty-nine ST Mk V, one hundred and thirty-three ST Mk VI and one hundred and seventeen GT Mk VI. These were further subdivided into Series according to variations of equipment or role. The eight ST Mk I Series 1's had only twin dorsal guns, with a sliding hood over them; the fourteen ST Mk I Series 2's had Malcolm glider-towing gear; the ST Mk VI's were Series 1's with a starboard side rear freight door; and the GT Mk VI's were Series 2's with additional radio equipment and no dorsal armament. The Mk II could operate as a 10-man paratroop transport, and the Mk V (otherwise similar to the Mk II) was fitted with fuel jettison equipment. All were powered by Bristol Hercules XI engines, though there was a project for a Merlin-engined Mk III, and one Mk IV was completed with 1,600 hp Wright R-2600-A5B Double Cyclones. Other RAF squadrons to operate the Albemarle included Nos 296 and 297 (in the United Kingdom and in North Africa), and No 570; small numbers also served with Nos 161 and 511, and some (ten?) Albemarles were supplied to the Soviet Air Force. Large numbers took part in the Allied landings in Sicily (July 1943), Normandy (June 1944) and at Arnhem (September 1944).

58 Beech UC-45 Expediter

This was the military version of the pre-war Beech Model 18, one of the most adaptable twin-engined aeroplanes ever built: developed versions are still in production, and operate in all parts of the world. First military orders were placed before Pearl Harbor, the U.S. Army ordering eleven 6-seat C-45's (Model B18S) and twenty 8-seat C-45A's in 1940-41. Also in 1941 came the first orders for a 5-seat navigation trainer version, the AT-7 Navigator, five hundred and seventy-seven of which were ultimately delivered. The first mass-produced military transport version was the C-45B, basically the same as the A but with interior layout modified to Army requirements. Two hundred and twenty-three C-45B's were produced for the USAAF, one hundred and twenty-one similar aircraft were supplied to Britain under Lend-Lease as Expediter Mk I's. Five went to the Royal Navy, the remainder to the RAF. The 'Utility Cargo' designation first appeared on the two UC-45C's adopted by the USAAF; the two UC-45D's and six UC-45E's were 5-seaters similar to the AT-7 and -7B trainers. Major production transport was the 7-seat UC-45F, one thousand one hundred and thirty-seven of which were delivered to the U.S. Army from 1944. An additional two hundred and thirty-six were supplied to the RAF, and sixty-seven to the Fleet Air Arm, by whom they were known as the Expediter II. Subsequent trainers included seven AT-7A's, with convertible twin float or ski landing gear, and nine AT-7B's, which were basically 'winterised' AT-7's. Five of this model were supplied to the RAF. Final USAAF variant was the AT-7C, with R-985-AN-3 engines; five hundred and forty-nine were completed. A development of the AT-7 for bombing training was the AT-11 Kansas, one thousand five hundred and eighty-two of which were completed; thirty-six were later converted to AT-11A's for navigation training. Many Expediters were used by the U.S. Navy, with JR (Utility Transport) series designations: the Navy's JRB-1, -2, -3 and -4 corresponded to the Army C-45, C-45A, C-45B and UC-45F respectively. Navy counterpart to the AT-7 was the SNB-2. Several other aircraft served as USAAF photographic aircraft, with the name Discoverer. These included fourteen F-2's, thirteen F-2A's (converted from transport models) and forty-two F-2B's.

59 Focke-Wulf Fw 189 Uhu (Owl)

The Fw 189 was designed originally to a 1937 specification for a tactical reconnaissance aircraft. The Fw 189V1 prototype (D-OPVN), first flown in July 1938, was an unorthodox aeroplane, with two 430 hp Argus As 410 engines mounted in slender booms that also carried the tail assembly. The crew members were accommodated in an extensively glazed central nacelle. A second and third prototype were completed to generally similar configuration, the Fw 189V2 carrying guns and external bomb racks. The first series version to go into production was the Fw 189B dual-control trainer, three B-0's and ten B-1's being completed in 1939-40. Production of the first reconnaissance series began in the spring of 1940, ten Fw 189A-0 pre-series aircraft being followed by the A-1, the better-armed A-2 and a smaller quantity of A-3 trainers. First deliveries to the *Luftwaffe* were made in the autumn of 1940, but it was not until the end of the following year that the Fw 189 began to appear in front-line units in any numbers. Thereafter the *Uhu*, as it was known to its crews, became employed in increasing numbers, especially on the Eastern Front. It was popular with those who flew it, and its delicate appearance belied what was in fact an adaptable, manoeuvrable and sturdily built aeroplane. Production of the Fw 189A series was undertaken by the parent company, which built one hundred and ninety-seven, excluding prototypes; at the Aero factory in Czechoslovakia, which built three hundred and thirty-seven; and at Bordeaux-Mérignac in France, where two hundred and ninety-three were completed. Small numbers were supplied to the air forces of Hungary and Slovakia. Meanwhile, in 1939 the Fw 189V1 had been reflown after being modified to have a very small but heavily armoured central nacelle seating two crew members. This and the generally similar Fw 189V6 were prototypes for a proposed attack version, the Fw 189C, but the latter did not go into production. The float-fitted Fw 189D, the Fw 189E with Gnome-

Rhône engines, and the more power-ful Fw 189G were all projects that did not come to fruition, but a small number of Fw 189F-1's, with 580 hp As 411 engines, did become opera-tional.

60 Blohm und Voss Bv 138

A product of Hamburger Flugzeug-bau, the aircraft division of the Blohm und Voss shipbuilding com-pany, the prototype of this three-engined flying boat was designated Ha 138V1 when it made its first flight on 15 July 1937. A second prototype, with a modified hull and tail surfaces, was flown on 6 Novem-ber 1937, both being powered by 600 hp Junkers Jumo 205C engines. In 1938 the 'Ha' designations were discarded, the third machine to be completed being designated Bv 138A-01. This was the first of six pre-production aircraft, embodying a much-enlarged hull, redesigned booms and tail, and a horizontal wing centre section. Production be-gan late in 1939 of twenty-five similar Bv 138A-1's, intended for well-equipped, long-range maritime patrol duties, but this initial version was not a conspicuous success, and the first pair were actually employed as 10-passenger transports in Nor-way. It made its combat debut in October 1940, at about which time the A-1 was beginning to be replaced by the Bv 138B-1, twenty-one of which were built with a turret-mounted nose cannon, a similar gun in the rear of the hull and 880 hp Jumo 205D engines. The major version in service was the Bv 138C-1, two hundred and twenty-seven of which

were produced between 1941 and 1943. The C-1, with more efficient propellers and a 13 mm upper gun, offered slightly better performance and defence than its predecessor. Despite an indifferent start to its career, the Bv 138 eventually proved to be both robust and versatile, and was employed with increasing effect both on convoy patrol in Arctic waters and, in association with the U-boat patrols, on anti-shipping missions over the North Atlantic and the Mediterranean. A few were also converted for sweeping or 'de-gaussing' minefields (these were designated Bv 138MS), and many more were adapted for launching from catapults.

61 C.R.D.A. Cant. Z.506B Airone (Heron)

The Z.506 first appeared as a 12-passenger commercial transport, the prototype (I-CANT) making its first flight in 1936 with Pratt & Whitney Hornet engines. Small batches of Z.506A's (760 hp Cyclones) and Z.506C's (750 or 800 hp Alfa Romeos) were delivered, from 1936 to 1938, to the Italian airline Ala Littoria, during which time suc-cessively improved world records for speed, distance and payload-to-height were established by various machines. Meanwhile, in July 1936 the prototype was handed over to the Italian Air Ministry, leading to the evolution of a bomber/torpedo bomber version, the Z.506B. This carried a crew of five and had a redesigned fuselage whose chief features were a raised cockpit, seat-ing the two pilots in tandem; a ventral gondola, incorporating a forward bomb aimer's position, the bomb bay and a rear defensive gun position; and a strut-braced tailplane. The bomb bay could accommodate two 1,102 lb (500 kg) bombs, various combinations of smaller bombs up to a total of 1,984 lb (900 kg) or a single 1,764 lb (800 kg) torpedo. A pair of Breda-SAFAT 12·7 mm machine-guns were installed in a retractable Breda M.1 dorsal turret. The Z.506B Serie I entered production at Monfalcone in 1937, thirty-two being completed and delivered to the *Regia Aeronautica* during 1938. Some of these joined Italy's *Aviazione Legionaria* in Spain at the end of that year, where they were employed primarily for rescue or reconnaissance missions. By June 1940 production at Monfalcone had reached ninety-five Serie I and later models, others had been completed by Piaggio at Finalmarina, and Z.506B's in Italian service included twenty-nine of an order for thirty placed by the Polish Government in 1938. Principal Airone formations in 1940 were the 31° *Stormo da Bombardamento Marittimo* at Elmas (Sardinia) and the 35° *Stormo B.M.* at Brindisi. The Airone was active in its primary role during the early part of the war, but after the Greek islands campaign of 1941 all aircraft of this type were diverted to maritime patrol duties of various kinds, serving, *inter alia*, with the 139°, 147°, 170° and 199° *Squadriglie da Ricognizione Marittimo*. After the Italian capitulation, twenty-three Z.506B's became part of the *Raggruppamento Idro* (seaplane group) of the Co-Belligerent Air Force based at Taranto. By this time the principal service variant was the Serie XII, the gross weight of which had been raised by improvements in bomb-carrying capacity (to 2,645 lb = 1,200 kg) and defensive armament. It has not been possible to establish individual details of intermediate Serie numbers, nor of overall Airone production. The only other wartime variant identified was the Z.506S (for Soccorso = help), a conversion of the Z.506B for air/sea rescue. Some of these served in *Luftwaffe* colours, five were among the Co-Belligerent Air Force's acquisitions in 1943, and a further twenty conversions were made by Siai-Marchetti after the war for the reconstituted *Aeronautica Militare Italiano*, with which they served until 1959.

62 Junkers Ju 52/3m

Although it first entered military service as a bomber, it is as a transport aeroplane that the Ju 52/3m began and ended its career. Developed from the single-engined Ju 52 flown in October 1930, the first of the Ju 52/3m trimotors made its maiden flight in 1932, and for several pre-war years they were used widely by Deutsche Lufthansa and other airlines, notably in South America. Several hundred were delivered to the *Luftwaffe* in 1934-35 in bomber configuration, but they were regarded only as interim equipment, pending the arrival of such types as the He 111 and Do 17. Thus, in their first operational role, in the Spanish Civil War of 1936-39, they were employed principally as troop transports. The early production models were powered by 600 hp BMW 132A engines; the first version to introduce the higher-powered BMW 132T was the Ju 53/3mg5e. Principal production model was the Ju 52/3mg7e, with enlarged cabin doors, autopilot and other detail improvements; this could be fitted out either as an 18-seat troop transport or as an ambulance with provision for 12 stretchers. In these two roles the Ju 52/3m served for many years with the *Luftwaffe*, by whom it was popularly known as 'Iron Annie'. Their best-known action came with the invasion of Norway in April 1940, in which nearly six hundred of these transports were engaged. Almost as many were in action during the invasion of France and the Low Countries, and in both campaigns well over a quarter of the Junkers transports involved were lost. Nevertheless, they continued to figure prominently in such subsequent Nazi campaigns as those in Greece, Libya and Crete. Other duties undertaken by the Ju 52/3m during its *Luftwaffe* career included those of supply transport and glider tug, and some aircraft were fitted with electromagnetic 'de-gaussing' rings for clearing minefields. Most models had provision for interchangeable wheel, ski or float landing gear. Overall production of the Ju 52/3m between 1934 and 1944, including civil models, amounted to four thousand eight hundred and forty-five aircraft. Of these, two thousand eight hundred and four were built in Germany between 1939 and 1945. Many pre-war commercial Ju 52/3m's were impressed for military service, and when the war was over several hundred were allocated to many foreign airlines, assisting them to re-establish their pre-war services until more modern types became available. A few remain in airline service today.

63 C.R.D.A. Cant. Z.1007 Alcione (Kingfisher)

The most important wartime contemporary of the S.M.79 Sparviero was another trimotor bomber, the Z.1007 designed by Ing Filippo Zappata. The first prototype flew towards the end of 1937, others following during the ensuing year and a half, and the Z.1007 entered production in 1939. The early aircraft for the *Regia Aeronautica* carried a light defensive armament of four 7·7 mm guns, and were powered by 840 hp Isotta-Fraschini Asso IX RC 35 Vee-type engines, installed in annular cowlings that gave them the appearance of being radials. This initial version was soon followed by the principal model, the Z.1007*bis*, in which a change was made to 1,000 hp Piaggio radials, resulting in a considerably improved performance. This version had increases in wing span and overall length, and a strengthened undercarriage, all permitting it to operate at higher gross weights; and defensive armament was improved. Eighty-seven Alcioni were in service when Italy entered the war. Of all-wood construction, the Alcione was unusual in being built in both single- and twin-finned forms; production was undertaken by IMAM

(Meridionali) and Piaggio, as well as by CRDA. As an alternative to its internal load, the Z.1007*bis* could carry a pair of 450 mm (17·7 in) torpedos under the fuselage, and the type was also employed for reconnaissance. The Alcione saw most of its wartime service in the Mediterranean area and North Africa, but also served on the Eastern Front, standing up well to extremes of climate despite its wooden construction. A later version, the Z.1007*ter*, appeared in *Regia Aeronautica* service towards the end of 1942. It had 1,175 hp Piaggio P.XIX engines and a reduced bomb load, but was not built in substantial numbers. The parallel Z.1015, with 1,500 hp Piaggio P.XII RC 35 engines, was likewise surpassed by the promise of an even better design, the Z.1018, which had flown in 1940.

64 Savoia-Marchetti S.M.79 Sparviero (Hawk)

The S.M.79, designed by Alessandro Marchetti, originated as the prototype (I-MAGO) of an 8-seat commercial transport, making its first flight in October 1934. Several record flights, with various powerplants, were made in 1935-36, leading to the completion of the second prototype as a military bomber, powered by three 780 hp Alfa Romeo 126 RC 34 engines. This entered production as the S.M.79-I Sparviero, characterised by the dorsal hump which caused it to be nicknamed *il Gobbo* (the hunchback) when it entered service. The 8° and 111° *Stormi Bombardamento Veloce* (High Speed Bomber Groups)

achieved some considerable success with their Sparvieri during the Spanish Civil War, and forty-five S.M.79-I's were ordered in 1938 by Yugoslavia. In 1937 service trials were begun of the S.M.79-I equipped to carry one 450 mm (17·7 in) torpedo, and later two, beneath the fuselage. These trials indicated that, with more powerful engines, the Sparviero could easily carry two of these weapons externally, and in October 1939 production began of the S.M.79-II, to equip the *Squadriglie Aerosiluranti* (Torpedo Bomber Squadrons) of the *Regia Aeronautica*. Apart from one batch with 1,030 hp Fiat A.80 RC 41 engines, all S.M.79-II's were powered by the Piaggio P.XI radial. Production was sub-contracted to Macchi and Reggiane factories, and in June 1940 there were nearly six hundred Sparvieri, of both models, in Italian service. The S.M.79 was active during World War 2 throughout the Mediterranean area, in North Africa and the Balkan states, its duties including torpedo attack, conventional bombing, reconnaissance, close-support and, eventually, transport and training. After the Italian surrender in 1943 about three dozen continued to fly with the Co-Belligerent Air Force, while the pro-German *Aviazione della RSI* employed several S.M.79-III's. This was a cleaned-up version, without the ventral gondola, and had a forward-firing 20 mm cannon. The S.M.79B was a twin-engined export model, with an extensively glazed nose, and was first flown in 1936. It was built for Brazil (three), Iraq

148

(four) and Rumania (forty-eight), each version with a different power-plant. The Rumanian I.A.R. factories also built the S.M.79B under licence with Junkers Jumo 211D in-line engines. Overall Italian production of S.M.79 variants, including export models, reached one thousand three hundred and thirty before output ceased in 1944.

65 Petlyakov Pe-8

The Pe-8 was evolved to meet a 1934 Soviet Air Force specification for a long range heavy bomber, and originally bore the designation ANT-42, indicating that it was a product of the A.N. Tupolev design bureau. Its military designation was TB-7. When the Soviet designation system was changed at the end of 1940 credit was given to Vladimir Petlyakov, who had led the team responsible for its design. The proto-type bomber first flew on 27 December 1936, with 1,100 hp Mikulin M-105 engines, and later trials were conducted with an M-100 engine mounted in the fuselage to drive a supercharger for the four propulsion engines. Late in 1939, when the TB-7 entered production at Kuznets, it was powered by AM-35A engines, which did not require this clumsy arrangement in order to maintain the bomber's excellent speed-at-altitude performance. The aircraft entered service during 1940, and in the summer of 1941 carried out their first major attack of the war when a formation of Pe-8's raided Berlin. They continued to make similar deep-penetration raids behind the German lines. Mean-while, attempts to improve the design had begun early in 1941 with the installation of M-30B diesel engines, whose greater fuel economy offered an even longer range. Unfortunately, this powerplant proved unsatisfactory in other ways, and trials with M-82 radials revealed an unacceptable loss of performance; eventually, the withdrawal from production of the AM-35A led to the installation, from 1943, of M-82FN fuel-injection radial engines in production Pe-8's. This version introduced various aero-dynamic improvements, evolved by I. F. Nyezval after Petlyakov's death in 1942, and the nacelle gun instal-lations were omitted. Design changes and powerplant difficulties were chiefly responsible for Pe-8 pro-duction coming to an end in 1944, the total number built being com-paratively small by Soviet wartime standards. In 1942 one Pe-8 made a flight of more than 11,000 miles (17,700 km) from Moscow to Washington and back via Scotland, Iceland and Canada.

66 Short Stirling

The Stirling was a victim of its own Specification (B.12/36), because of which its wings were of such low aspect ratio that its operational ceiling was limited and its bomb bay could take no single weapon larger than 2,000 lb (907 kg) in size. The prototype (L 7600), preceded in 1938 by flight trials of the P.31 half-scale wooden prototype, made its first flight on 14 May 1939. It crashed on landing, but a second machine (L 7605) was flown on

3 December 1939. In May 1940 the first production Stirling Mk I made its maiden flight, and deliveries of this version began in August 1940 to No 7 Squadron. The initial order for one hundred Stirlings was soon increased, and after the 1939 Munich crisis stood at one thousand five hundred. Hercules XI engines of 1,595 hp in the Mk I replaced the 1,375 hp Hercules II's of the two prototypes. Two conversions were made as Mk II prototypes, with 1,600 hp Wright R-2600-A5B Cyclone engines, but this model never went into production. The major service version was the Mk III, which in addition to Hercules XVI engines introduced a new-style dorsal gun turret. Two Mk III's were converted in 1943 as Mk IV prototypes, the latter version being produced for both paratroop transport and glider towing duties. The Mk IV was basically similar to the Mk III, except for the removal of some or all gun turrets and having, in the paratrooper version, an exit hatch aft of the bomb bay. The final version, the Mk V, was an unarmed passenger or cargo transport with a fuselage rear-loading door and an extended nose section which hinged sideways to provide an additional loading facility. Short Bros built five hundred and thirty-two Mk I, six hundred and eighteen Mk III, four hundred and fifty Mk IV and one hundred and sixty Mk V; in addition, one hundred and ninety-one Mk I and four hundred and twenty-nine Mk II were completed by Austin Motors. The Stirling I first went into action on 10 February

1941, with an attack on an oil storage depot at Rotterdam, and throughout 1942 began mounting the heavy bombing of enemy targets later continued by the Halifax and Lancaster by night and the U.S. Fortress and Liberator by day. It figured in the first and many subsequent thousand-bomber raids, and was the first Bomber Command type fitted with the 'Oboe' blind-bombing device. Before their transfer to less belligerent duties in the later war years many Stirlings also carried out minelaying duties.

67 Focke-Wulf Fw 200 Condor

The Fw 200V1 prototype (D-AERE *Saarland*), which first flew on 27 July 1937, was designed by Dr Kurt Tank as a 26-passenger commercial transport for Deutsche Lufthansa, and prior to World War 2 the Fw 200A and Fw 200B also served with Danish and Brazilian operators. Two other prototypes were acquired by the RLM, later becoming personal transports for Hitler and his staff, but the first suggestion to employ the Condor for maritime patrol came from Japan. None of the aircraft ordered by Japan were in fact delivered, but the Condor was adapted, as the Fw 200C, for ocean patrol and bombing duties with the *Luftwaffe*. In spite of this it was as a military transport that the Fw 200C was first employed operationally, during the invasion of Norway in the spring of 1940. Early production Fw 200C's were powered by 830 hp BMW 132H engines and carried a crew of 5, but with successive variations in armament the crew later increased to 7 men, and from the Fw 200C-3 onward Bramo 323R engines became the standard power-plant. The Fw 200C-1 first entered service in the maritime role towards the end of 1940, with *Kampfgeschwader* 40, followed by the C-2 and C-3 models during 1941. The principal sub-type was the C-4, with more advanced radar and radio equipment, which entered production early in 1942. Subsequent variants included the C-6 and C-8, adapted to carry two Hs 293 guided missiles. The latter was the final military variant, a total of two hundred and seventy-six Condors (including prototypes) having been built when production ended early in 1944. Considering the small quantity built, the Condor established a considerable reputation as a commerce raider during the early war years, operating independently or in conjunction with U-boat patrols against the Allied convoys. It was not ideally suited to the rigours of maritime warfare, however, and many were lost through structural failure when indulging in strenuous manoeuvres. When its initial successes began to diminish after the appearance of the CAM ships and such Allied types as the Beaufighter and Liberator, it was progressively transferred to the transport role for which it had first been designed.

68 & 69   Boeing B-17 Fortress

In service from beginning to end of the U.S. participation in World War 2, the B-17 was evolved in 1934 for a USAAC design competition for an offshore anti-shipping bomber. In 1935 the prototype was completed, as the Boeing 299, and flew for the first time on 28 July 1935, powered by four 750 hp Pratt & Whitney Hornet engines. A change of power-plant, to 930 hp Wright Cyclones, was specified for the thirteen Y1B-17's and one Y1B-17A that were then ordered for evaluation; after trials, these were placed in service as the B-17 and B-17A respectively. The initial production batch comprised thirty-nine B-17B's, with modified nose, larger rudder and internal improvements. They were followed by thirty-eight B-17C's (higher-powered Cyclones and revised armament), twenty of which were supplied to the Royal Air Force in 1941 as the Fortress Mk I. The B-17D, forty-two of which were ordered for the USAAF, was generally similar, and the American C's were later converted to D standard. It was the B-17E which first introduced the huge, sail-like fin and rudder that character-ised all subsequent Fortresses, and the much-improved defensive armament on this model included, for the first time, a tail gun turret to cover the blind spot to the rear of the bomber. Five hundred and twelve B-17E's were built by Boeing, including forty-five which became the Fortress IIA of the RAF. American B-17E's, serving in the United Kingdom, made the first raids on European targets by the U.S. Eighth Air Force in August 1942, and this version also served extensively in the Pacific theatre. The next model, the B-17F, was sub-contracted to Douglas and

Lockheed-Vega factories which, with Boeing, manufactured three thousand of this model. Nineteen of these were supplied to the RAF as the Fortress II, and sixty-one others were converted to F-9 series photographic reconnaissance aircraft. The same three companies combined to build eight thousand six hundred and eighty examples of the last production model, the B-17G; eighty-five of these became Fortress III's with RAF Coastal Command and ten others were converted to F-9C's. The B-17G was characterised chiefly by its 'chin' turret with two additional 0·50 in machine-guns, a feature later added to several B-17F's in service. Forty B-17G's were allocated to the U.S. Navy, with whom they performed anti-submarine or early warning patrol duties; these aircraft were designated PB-1G or PB-1W respectively, the latter having large ventral radomes. About one hundred and thirty other Fortresses, adapted to carry a lifeboat under the fuselage, were redesignated B-17H and employed on air/sea rescue work. The Fortress's principal sphere of activity during World War 2 was in Europe, where the E, F and G models were the mainstay of the U.S. heavy day bomber attacks on enemy targets.

70 **Boeing B-29 Superfortress**
Design of the Superfortress began well before America's entry into World War 2, when the Boeing Model 345 was evolved to a USAAC requirement of February 1940 for a 'hemisphere defense weapon'. In August 1940 two prototypes, designated XB-29, were ordered by the USAAF, and the first one was flown on 21 September 1942. It was a much larger aeroplane than Boeing's earlier B-17 Fortress, and was characterised by its circular-section, pressurised fuselage and remote-controlled gun turrets. Powerplant was four 2,200 hp Wright R-3350-13 Cyclone radial engines. By the time of the first flight, nearly seventeen hundred B-29's had been ordered. The first pre-production YB-29 Superfortress flew on 26 June 1943, and squadron deliveries began in the following month to the 58th Bombardment Wing. The first operational B-29 mission was carried out on 5 June 1944, and the first attack upon a target in Japan on 15 June 1944. It was during this month that the Superfortresses moved to the bases in the Marianas Islands, from whence they subsequently mounted a steadily increasing bombing campaign against the Japanese homeland. Apart from the direct damage caused by this campaign, it was responsible for many Japanese aircraft from other Pacific battle fronts being withdrawn for home defence duties, although comparatively few types were capable of indulging in effective combat at the altitudes flown by the American bombers. Superfortresses also carried out extensive minelaying in Japanese waters, and others were employed as F-13A photographic reconnaissance aircraft. Finally, two B-29's brought the war to its dramatic close with the dropping of atomic bombs on Hiroshima and Nagasaki on 6 and 9 August 1945. Shortly after VJ-day

over five thousand Superfortresses were cancelled, but when B-29 production ended early in 1946 the three Boeing factories had completed two thousand seven hundred and sixty-six B-29's and B-29A's; in addition, six hundred and sixty-eight B-29's were manufactured by Bell, and five hundred and thirty-six B-29's by Martin. Three hundred and eleven of the Bell machines were later converted to B-29B's with reduced armament.

71 Avro Lancaster

The Lancaster was a direct development of Avro's unsuccessful Manchester twin-engined bomber, its prototype (BT 308) being originally the Manchester III, complete with triple tail unit, modified by the installation of four 1,130 hp Merlin X engines in place of the two Vulture engines of the Manchester. This prototype flew on 9 January 1941, being followed just over nine months later by the first production Mk I, of which delivery began (to No 44 Squadron) shortly after Christmas 1941. The first Lancaster combat mission came on 2 March 1942, and the first bombing raid, on Essen, followed eight days later. The Lancaster I, fitted successively with Merlin XX, 22 or 24 engines, remained the only version in service throughout 1942 and early 1943, and an eventual total of three thousand four hundred and forty Mk I's were completed by Avro, Armstrong Whitworth, Austin Motors, Metropolitan-Vickers and Vickers-Armstrongs. Avro completed two prototypes for the Lancaster II, powered

by 1,725 hp Bristol Hercules radial engines as a safeguard against possible supply shortage of Merlins. In the event no such shortage arose, but three hundred production Lancaster II's were built by Armstrong Whitworth. The other principal version, the Lancaster III, was powered by Packard-built Merlin 28, 38 or 224 engines; apart from a modified bomb-aimer's window, this exhibited few other differences from the Mk I. Most of the three thousand and twenty Mk III's completed were built by Avro, but one hundred and ten were manufactured by Armstrong Whitworth and one hundred and thirty-six by Metropolitan-Vickers. The Mark numbers IV and V applied to extensively redesigned models that eventually became the Lincoln, while the small batch of Mk VI's were Mk III's converted to Merlin 85 or 87 engines in redesigned cowlings. The final British variant was the Mk VII, one hundred and eighty being built by Austin with Martin dorsal turrets mounting twin 0·50 in guns. In Canada, Victory Aircraft Ltd manufactured four hundred and thirty Lancaster X's, which had Packard-Merlin 28's and were essentially similar to the Mk III. The Lancaster's bomb-carrying feats were legion. It was designed originally to carry bombs of 4,000 lb (1,814 kg) in size, but successive modifications to the bomb bay produced the Mk I (Special) capable of carrying first 8,000 lb (3,629 kg) and then 12,000 lb (5,443 kg) weapons, and culminating in the 22,000 lb (9,979 kg) 'Grand Slam' armour-piercing weapon designed by Barnes Wallis. This remarkable engineer also designed the skipping bomb carried by the Lancasters of No 617 Squadron in their epic raid on the Moehne and Eder dams on 17 May 1943.

72 & 73 Handley Page Halifax

The H.P.57 came into being as a redesign of the twin-Vulture-engined H.P.56 evolved to meet Air Ministry Specification P.13/36, after it had become apparent that the Vulture would be unsatisfactory. The H.P.57 was a much-enlarged design, drawn up around four Rolls-Royce Merlin engines, and the first of two prototypes (L 7244) was flown on 24 September 1939, by which time an initial contract had already been placed. Deliveries of the Halifax Mk I, to No 35 Squadron, began in November 1940, and the bomber made its operational debut in a raid on Le Havre on the night of 11-12 March 1941. The early machines became known as Mk I Series I, being followed by the Mk I Series II with a higher gross weight and Series III with increased fuel tankage. The first major modification appeared in the Mk II Series I, with its two-gun dorsal turret and uprated Merlin XX engines. The Mk II Series I (Special) had a fairing in place of the nose turret, and the engine exhaust muffs omitted; the Series IA first introduced the drag-reducing moulded Perspex nose that became a standard Halifax feature, had a four-gun dorsal turret, and Merlin 22 engines. Variants of the Mk II Series I (Special) and Series IA, with Dowty landing gear instead of the

standard Messier gear, were designated Mk V Series I (Special) and Series IA. One thousand nine hundred and sixty-six Mk II's and nine hundred and fifteen Mk V's were built. One other important modification appearing in the Mk II Series IA was the introduction of larger, rectangular vertical tail surfaces, designed to overcome serious control difficulties experienced with earlier models. The Perspex nose and rectangular fins characterised all subsequent Halifaxes, whose only serious drawback now was a lack of adequate power. Thus, in the Mk III, which appeared in 1943, the Merlin powerplant was abandoned in favour of Bristol Hercules radial engines. The Mk III became the most numerous Halifax variant, two thousand and ninety-one being built. The Mk IV was a project that remained uncompleted, the next operational models being the Mks VI and VII, the former powered by 1,675 hp Hercules 100, while the latter reverted to the Hercules XVI as used in the Mk III. These were the final bomber versions, and compared with earlier models were built in relatively small numbers. Halifax production ended with the Mk VIII supply transport and Mk IX paratroop transport, the final aircraft being delivered in November 1946. Six thousand one hundred and seventy-six Halifaxes had then been built, by a widely sub-contracted wartime programme that included English Electric, Fairey, Rootes Motors and the London Aircraft Production Group as well as the parent company. The Halifax remained in service with Bomber Command throughout the war, making its last operational sortie on 25 April 1945. Its work included many special-duty missions, including agent-dropping and radar countermeasures, and it also served in the Middle East. After the war Halifaxes remained in service for a time with Coastal and Transport Commands, the last flight being made by a Coastal Command GR Mk VI in March 1952.

74 & 75 Consolidated B-24 Liberator

To the Liberator go the distinctions of being built in greater numbers and more variants than any other U.S. aircraft of World War 2, and of serving in more combat theatres, over a longer period, than any heavy bomber on either side. It originated as the Consolidated Model 32, a major feature of which was the exceptionally high aspect ratio Davis wing that gave the Liberator its prodigious range. Allied to this was the deep, capacious fuselage that enabled the aircraft to carry a large bomb load and also made it eminently suitable as a transport. The sole XB-24 prototype flew on 29 December 1941, followed by seven YB-24 service trials aircraft and thirty-six production B-24A's. One hundred and twenty were also ordered by the French Government, but these were diverted to Britain, the first few being designated LB-30 or -30A and used by BOAC for transatlantic ferry flying. Twenty others went to RAF Coastal Command as Liberator I's, equipped with an early form of ASV

radar. The first B-24A deliveries to the USAAF were made in June 1941, followed by nine B-24C's with turbo-supercharged engines and revised armament. The first U.S. version actually to serve in the bomber role was the B-24D, which was essentially similar to the B-24C except for its R-1830-43 engines and increased gross weight. Production of the B-24D, including ten by Douglas, totalled two thousand seven hundred and thirty-eight. Two hundred and sixty were supplied to the RAF as the Liberator III and IIIA (the former having Boulton Paul gun turrets), plus a further one hundred and twenty-two, fitted with 'chin' and ventral radar fairings and Leigh airborne searchlights, which served with Coastal Command as the Liberator Mk V. In mid-1943 those USAAF B-24D's engaged on anti-submarine patrol were transferred to the U.S. Navy, by whom they were redesignated PB4Y-1. Seven hundred and ninety-one B-24E's were built by Convair (as Consolidated was now known), Douglas and the Ford Motor Co, distinguishable from the D model chiefly by their modified propellers; while North American contributed four hundred and thirty B-24G's, some of them with a powered gun turret installed in the nose. An Emerson nose turret and R-1830-65 engines characterised the B-24H, three thousand one hundred of which were completed by Convair, Douglas and Ford. These three companies, plus North American, then manufactured six thousand six hundred and seventy-eight B-24J's, with a Motor Products nose turret and a ventral Briggs ball turret. One thousand two hundred and seventy-eight B-24J's became the RAF's Liberator Mk VI bomber and Mk VII for general reconnaissance. Nine hundred and seventy-seven were delivered to the U.S. Navy, also receiving the designation PB4Y-1 and having, in most cases, radar in place of the ventral turret. Other armament variations characterised the B-24L (one thousand six hundred and sixty-seven by Convair and Ford) and B-24M (two thousand five hundred and ninety-three, from the same factories). Ford had completed seven examples of the single-finned YB-24N, and forty-six similar RY-3's which were delivered to the U.S. Navy, when further contracts (for over five thousand B-24N's) were cancelled in May 1945. The Liberator, although sharing a substantial part of the bombing of Europe with its contemporary, the Boeing Fortress, was even more prominent in the Pacific theatre, where its excellent range was particularly valuable. It also gave considerable service as a transport aircraft, two hundred and seventy-six B-24D-type aircraft being completed as C-87's for this role; close on one hundred Liberators of various types were adapted as F-7 series photo-reconnaissance aircraft; and others were utilised as cargo transports, tanker aircraft and flying classrooms. In addition to those serving with the U.S. forces and the RAF, considerable numbers also operated with the Canadian and other Commonwealth air forces.

When Liberator production ended on 31 May 1945 the total output of all variants had reached eighteen thousand one hundred and eighty-eight aircraft.

76 Short Sunderland

The Sunderland, eventually to become the RAF's longest-serving operational aircraft, was first delivered to No 230 Squadron in Singapore early in June 1938. Its design, based upon the successful C Class 'Empire' flying boats of Imperial Airways, was evolved to Specification R.2/33, and the prototype (K 4774) was flown on 16 October 1937 with 950 hp Pegasus X engines. With Pegasus XXII's and revised nose and tail armament, the Sunderland Mk I entered production in 1938, and by 3 September 1939 forty were in service with four RAF squadrons. Ninety Mk I's were eventually completed, including fifteen by Blackburn. This company also built five of the forty-three Sunderland II's which, from the end of 1941, began to replace the Mk I's in service. The Mk II introduced Pegasus XVIII engines, with two-stage superchargers, a twin-gun Botha-type dorsal turret in place of the 'midships gun ports, an improved tail turret and ASV radar. Rising operating weights now necessitated redesign of the hull planing bottom, and the Mk II on which this was tested thus became the prototype for the chief production model, the Sunderland III. The first Short-built Mk III flew on 15 December 1941; the parent company eventually produced two hundred and eighty-six Mk III's, while a further one hundred and seventy were built by Blackburn. It was No 10 Squadron of the Royal Australian Air Force which first experimented with a group of four machine-guns in the nose of the Sunderland III. This proved so successful, both against enemy submarines and aircraft, that many Sunderlands were subsequently operated with this total armoury of ten guns, their bristling defence earning them the respectful nickname *Stachelschwein* (porcupine) from their German adversaries. The designation Sunderland IV was given originally to a larger, heavier development with 1,700 hp Bristol Hercules engines, eight 0·50 in machine-guns, and two 20 mm cannon. In the event, only two prototypes and eight production aircraft were built; they were given the new type name Seaford, but after a brief service appearance were later converted into Solent commercial transports for BOAC. Final military variant was the Mk V (one hundred built by Shorts and fifty by Blackburn), with 1,200 hp Pratt & Whitney R-1830-90 Twin Wasps as powerplant and improved ASV equipment. The Sunderland V entered service in February 1945, and was the last version to serve with the RAF, finally retiring in 1958. Sunderlands exported post-war to the French *Aéronavale* (nineteen) and the RNZAF (sixteen) served until 1960 and 1966 respectively.

77 Kawanishi H8K

The 13-Shi (1938) specification to which Dr Kikuhara designed the first prototype H8K1 was an exacting one, and in its initial trials early in 1941 the flying boat gave little indication of its future promise, having a lack of stability on the water and a marked tendency to 'porpoise'. Various modifications were made to this and the three pre-production H8K1's of 1941, all of which were powered by 1,530 hp Mitsubishi Kasei 11 engines. As finally accepted for production in February 1942, the H8K1 Model 11 had a deeper hull, with a more efficient planing bottom, and enlarged vertical tail surfaces. Thirteen production H8K1's were built at Kohnan. They carried a crew of 10 and were armed, like the pre-series machines, with a single 20 mm tail gun, one 20 mm and two 7·7 mm guns in the nose turret and a 7·7 mm gun in each of the beam blisters. Operational debut of 'Emily', as the H8K was later dubbed by the Allies, was made by the three pre-series H8K1's. These made an abortive attack on Pearl Harbor early in March 1942, flying from the Marshall Islands and refuelling from submarine tankers *en route*. The production H8K1 was an excellent hydrodynamic design, with a performance equal or superior to any other flying boat in service during the war. In 1943 it was superseded by the H8K2 Model 12, with more powerful Kasei 22 engines and increased armament. This was employed throughout the Pacific theatre, its maximum endurance of nearly 27 hours enabling it to carry out extremely long range maritime patrol, bombing and reconnaissance duties. Late production H8K2's carried ASV radar in the bow, the beam observation blisters being omitted. One hundred and twelve H8K2's were completed during 1943-45, plus thirty-six examples of a transport version, the H8K2-L Model 32 Sei-Ku (Clear Sky). This could carry up to sixty-four passengers, or a mixed load of passengers and cargo. It was recognisable by double rows of fuselage windows and a reduced armament of a single 13 mm and 20 mm gun respectively in the nose and tail. The first prototype H8K1, re-engined in 1943 with Kasei 22's and converted to a passenger layout, served as the trials aircraft for this version. Two H8K3 Model 22's were essentially late production H8K2's fitted experimentally with retractable wing-tip floats (originally planned for the first prototype) and a retractable dorsal turret. Later they were re-engined with Kasei 25b's and were redesignated H8K4 Model 23. Neither went into production, and the projected H8K4-L Model 33 transport was never completed.

78 **Kawanishi H6K**

One of the most efficient Japanese aircraft of the late 1930's, the Kawanishi H6K flying boat was designed to a JNAF specification of 1934, and three of the five prototypes had flown by the end of 1936. Two of these, and one other machine, had their original 840 hp Nakajima Hikari 2 engines replaced later by 1,000 hp Mitsubishi Kinsei 43's, in which form they were delivered to the JNAF for squadron service in

January 1938 under the designation H6K1. The fifth machine served as prototype for the initial production version, the H6K2 Model 11, nine more of which were built. The designation H6K3 was allocated to the next two aircraft, which were completed as transports. They were later restyled H6K2-L, and a total of eighteen was eventually delivered to Japan Air Lines as 16-seat commercial and military transports. The early military models flew operationally with the JNAF during the Sino-Japanese conflict, but by the outbreak of World War 2 the principal version in service was the H6K4 Model 22. Initially, this had been built with Kinsei 43 engines, but from August 1941 the standard powerplant became the more powerful Kinsei 46, permitting higher operating weights. Sixty-six Model 22's, later code-named 'Mavis' by the Allies, were in JNAF service at the time of Pearl Harbor, and eventually between two and three times this number were completed, several of them as H6K4-L transports. An attempt to prolong the flying boat's career resulted in the H6K5 Model 23, with 1,300 hp Kinsei 53 engines, but the satisfactory evolution of the later H8K from the same stable rendered such a course unnecessary, and only a comparatively small number of H6K5's were built. Most 'Mavis' flying boats ended their careers in the transport role, but by the end of 1943 they had virtually disappeared from service. A total of two hundred and seventeen H6K's, of all versions, were built.

79 Messerschmitt Me 323

Messerschmitt's huge transport glider, the Me 321 *Gigant*, had been produced only in small numbers before it was realised that the need to use rocket assistance and three twin-engined Bf 110's to get it into the air was uneconomical. Ing Degel of Messerschmitt was therefore given, early in 1941, the task of evolving from it an aeroplane that could take off under its own power. His solution, calculated also to avoid making demands upon German engine production, was to install Gnome-Rhône 14N engines, already in production in Occupied France. At first it was supposed that four of these engines would suffice, and ten prototypes were completed to this configuration. The first, designated Me 323V1, was flown in April 1941, but it soon became apparent that four engines were inadequate, and in August 1941 the first of five six-engined prototypes was flown. When manufacture of the Me 321 glider ended in January 1942, the six-engined Me 323 entered production. The initial model was the Me 323D-1, of which just over two dozen were built. One example was also completed of the Me 323D-2, to compare the merits of two-blade wooden propellers with the three-blade metal ones of the D-1. The D-1's five MG 131 machine-guns remained the minimum basic armament of the main production model, the Me 323D-6. However, additional weapons were often carried, and there were reports of some Me 323's with as many as eighteen machine-guns on board. In 1943 one hundred and forty

Me 323D-6's were built, and Messerschmitt delivered nineteen examples of the Me 323E-1, whose basic armament included a power-operated turret, mounting a 20 mm MG 151 cannon, installed above the centre engine nacelle on each wing. In 1944, before having to devote its resources to the Me 262 jet fighter, Messerschmitt had begun production of the Me 323F-1, powered by Gnome-Rhône 14R engines. Production was then transferred to the Zeppelin plant at Friedrichshafen, where a few F-1's were re-engined in mid-1944 with 1,340 hp Jumo 211F engines, but little further output was undertaken. The Me 323 was an invaluable supply transport on the Eastern Front, where it first appeared, but in North Africa and elsewhere its slow speed and difficult handling made it an easy prey for Allied fighters. After heavy losses during the evacuation of Tunisia little more was heard of this huge aeroplane, and further projected versions remained uncompleted.

80 Yokosuka MXY-7 Ohka (Cherry Blossom)

Most Japanese *Kamikaze* (Divine Wind) suicide air attacks were made by existing service aircraft adapted for the purpose, but one aircraft developed specifically for this role was also met operationally. This was the Ohka piloted flying bomb, developed to a project initiated by the Japanese Naval Air Research and Development Centre and evolved by the Yokosuka Naval Air Arsenal. Design work began in August 1944, priority production by several factories starting in September. The only version to reach combat status was the Model 11, seven hundred and fifty-five of which were built up to March 1945. Powered by a three-barrelled rocket motor and carrying a 2,645 lb (1,200 kg) warhead in the nose, the Ohka was attached beneath the belly of a G4M2e parent aircraft, the bomb doors of which were removed in order to accommodate it. The Ohka was carried to about 50 miles (80 km) from its target, when it was launched from a height usually around 27,000 ft (8,200 km) at an airspeed of some 200 mph (320 km/hr) to complete its journey alone. The pilot maintained it in a glide towards the target, using the rocket motor only for the last few miles and the ultimate steep dive. Fifty Ohka Model 11's were aboard the carrier *Shinano* when it was sunk by U.S. forces *en route* to the Philippines in November 1944. The aircraft was first encountered operationally on 21 March 1945, when sixteen Ohkas, with their parent aircraft and an escort of thirty Zero fighters, were intercepted while making for a U.S. task force about 300 miles (480 km) from Kyushu. All of the Ohka-carrying bombers, and half of the escorting fighters, were destroyed without a single weapon being launched. Sub-sequently, about three hundred Ohkas were allocated to the Okinawa area; probably no more than a quarter of these were launched at Allied targets, but these were enough to persuade their victims, at least, that perhaps the code name *Baka* (Japanese for 'fool') bestowed by the U.S. Navy was after all something of a misnomer. The only other version built in quantity was the Model 22, about fifty of which were completed. This had a 13 ft 6¼ in (4·12 m) wing span, was 22 ft 6⅞ in (6·88m) long, and had a gross weight of 3,197 lb (1,450 kg) including a 1,323 lb (600 kg) warhead. Powerplant was a TSU-11 jet engine, the compressor of which was driven by a 110 hp Hatsukaze piston-engine to provide 441 lb (200 kg) of thrust. The intended parent aircraft was the P1Y1 Ginga, but the Ohka 22 had a disappointing performance and did not go into service. The Model 33, proposed in April 1945, was incomplete when the war ended. Intended for air-launching from the G8N1 Renzan four-engined bomber, it would have had a 1,047 lb (475 kg) st Ne-20 turbojet and a warhead comparable to the Model 11. Project studies were also made for Models 43A (with folding wings) and 43B, to be launched from submarine-based and land-based catapults respectively.

INDEX

Heinkel	He 111	23	39	115
	He 115	21	37	113
	He 177 Greif	43	59	132
Ilyushin	Il-4 (DB-3F)	25	41	116
Junkers	Ju 52/3m	62	78	146
	Ju 87	19	35	111
	Ju 88	31	47	121
Kawanishi	H6K	78	94	158
	H8K	77	93	157
Lockheed	Hudson	54	70	140
	Lodestar	56	72	142
	Ventura	55	71	141
Martin	A-30 Baltimore	34	50	124
	B-26 Marauder	35	51	125
	Model 167 Maryland	26	42	117
Messerschmitt	Me 323	79	95	159
Mitsubishi	G4M	38	54	127
	Ki-21	37	53	126
	Ki-46	41	57	130
	Ki-67 Hiryu	39	55	128
Nakajima	B5N	10	26	104
	B6N Tenzan	16	32	109
	C6N Saiun	20	36	112
	Ki-49 Donryu	40	56	129
Noorduyn	Norseman	4	20	99
North American	B-25 Mitchell	53	69	139
Petlyakov	Pe-8 (TB-7)	65	81	149
PZL	P.37 Łoś	36	52	125
Saab	Saab-18	47	63	135
Savoia-Marchetti	S.M.79 Sparviero	64	80	148
Short	Stirling	66	82	149
	Sunderland	76	92	156
Sukhoi	Su-2	14	30	107
Supermarine	Walrus	1	17	97
Vickers	Wellington	22	38	114
Westland	Lysander	5	21	99
Yokosuka	D4Y Suisei	12	28	106
	MXY-7 Ohka	80	96	159
	P1Y1 Ginga	42	58	131